MW00721045

THE WORLD
OF LAOZI

THE WORLD OF LAOZI

Lectures on the Daodejing

Published by Seoul Selection U.S.A., Inc.
4199 Campus Dr., Suite 550, Irvine, CA 92612
Phone: 949-509-6584 / Seoul office: 82-2-734-9567
Fax: 949-509-6599 / Seoul office: 82-2-734-9562
Email: hankinseoul@gmail.com
Website: www.seoulselection.com
Printed in the Republic of Korea

ISBN: 978-1-62412-115-9 53000

Library of Congress Control Number: 2018954337

THE WORLD
OF LAOZI

Prime Dharma Master Kyongsan

Seoul Selection

Contents

Do You See? The Way Is Here

Liking is higher than knowing, we are told, and enjoying is deeper than liking. Can I say that I know Laozi? Is my appreciation at the level of liking or at the stage of enjoying? Perhaps I am someone who would make a sincere commitment to try to understand well.

It was the winter vacation after my first year in college, when my first encounter with the *Daodejing* (*Scripture of the Way and Virtue*) began, after I pled the dharma master Gangsan to teach it to me.

It was an unusually cold winter. I read *Daodejing* out loud, looking up unfamiliar Chinese characters in the dictionary. I had a feeling of being pulled into some profound place, and a vague sense of a superior person of transcendent character. I didn't grasp the whole meaning of the book at the time, but I was fascinated by Laozi.

I had sometimes taken the *Caigentan* along with me on journeys before, but now I found myself bringing the *Daodejing*. Afterward I read a number of translations, including in the *Daodejing* annotated by Kim Gyeong-tak, and I also had a few opportunities to learn the *Daodejing* from others. On one occasion, I was advised by someone to read it carefully, and I did so. Later, I gave a few lectures to students under the title "Reading the Classics." My encounters with Laozi's *Daodejing* had a long history, and I had had no shortage of opportunities to study it. But because I had been focused more on understanding the content than on a verbal interpretation of the Chinese text, I must state now that it would have been beyond me to attempt a traditional or word-to-word interpretation.

If my image of Zhuangzi is that of a liberated man wandering freely outside the domain of this world, then my sense of Laozi is of someone who may be liberated as well but who is not a statesman who governs the world; rather, his moderated and refined nature gives the sense of true maturity. It is as though one is meeting an old, greatly experienced, and skilled man who neither clutches nor casts aside this great object that we call the world, yet who handles it in just the right way.

It is truly extraordinary to imagine how just one book could become the object of contemplation by so many people over so many years, or how immense an influence it could cast on the lives of all of those different manifestations of philosophy, politics, culture, history, and humanity. A scripture comes to affect lives as it is read by students and organizations and rendered into a philosophy. It is truly amazing, then, to consider that Laozi had no organization, nor did he have an organized body of students.

Founding Master Sotaesan, Park Jung-bin, once said that the dimensions of heaven and earth were determined so as "to make and pass down clothes that fit each human being." We can understand this to mean that we are obliged to recreate the people and systems of the past in a way that is suited to today—to keep them alive and to share their words.

What would Laozi teach us or say to us if he were to arrive at this point in history, an age of science as symbolized by the computer, an age of the "global village," an age of equality, and an age of human rights? It is certainly a question worth considering.

We need the wisdom to reinterpret the *Daodejing* in a way that is suited to these times. I would like to offer such an interpretation, sharing its familiar wisdom with our political leaders, our educators, and our common people with shopping baskets in tow.

It seems to me that we have long understood the *dao* (the Way) shared by Laozi as something too lofty, too much like a form of playing with ideas.

I believe that now is the time for us to draw the *daode* (the Way and its virtue) that Laozi described to us as part of the reality closest to us, to devote our passion to living the nameless Way and the virtue of nonaction. It should not be the *Daodejing* as a pie-in-the-sky ideal but spiritual food in our daily lives. It should be a scripture for practical use that can nurture our working and family lives. For this purpose, I have strived to explain the *Daodejing* in such a way that its teaching can be easily applicable to our lives.

My earnest hope is that you read *Daodejing* over and over, and contemplate its meaning again and again so that the Way of old Laozi becomes your Way and you become a seeker of the Way, a practitioner of the Way, and a master of Way, not only enriching your own life but also steering the world toward right directions.

The sky is empty and the land is silent.
Plants and grasses are blue and green and the animals roam the
  fields.
The world's rise and fall ripples like a wave.
Try to say
Where is the Way among these?
Tell me!
The identity of the Way is truly unknown.
One cannot find its traces
Nor can one see its image.

Yet by accepting the teachings of prophets
After seeking, seeking, and seeking again
Once the mind's eye opens,

In the Great Void of the boundless heaven,
The sun and moon come and go.
On the vast expanse of earth,
The myriad things all boast their forms.
Within the long and limitless time,
All things in the world rise and fall by reason.
Within the long and limitless years
There is nothing that is not the Way, nothing that is not virtuous.

Do you see? The Way is here.
Do you understand? The Virtue is here.

With hands in prayer,
Jang Eung-cheol

Truth, That Which Cannot Be Named

Truth that can be conceived in thought
Cannot be called absolute truth.
Truth that can be expressed in words
Cannot be called eternal truth.

Truth that cannot be fully expressed in a name
Is the ground of heaven and earth.
Principles that can be expressed in words
Are the mother that nurtures all things in the universe.

Only the stage of no-thought comes home to one's heart
Can one realize the ultimate truth.
Only through engaging in mindful contemplation
Can one understand the myriad principles of transformation.

Truth that cannot be named
Is originally one with principles that can be named,
Though we call them by different names according to occasion.

One great truth,
Profound and mysterious,
Is the gateway that contains all of the myriad marvelous principles.

The words in this first chapter represent the core content of the *Daodejing*. Like a lantern for this scripture, they articulate the substance and function of the truth that operates all things in heaven and on earth, the way to experience them, and the profundity of the one truth.

The overall content of the *Daodejing* provides a concrete interpretation of the words in the first chapter, sharing the process of adopting them in one's character and the feelings of the sage who has achieved completion through practice, as well as the way he or she lives life, his or her wisdom living in this world, his or her political capabilities and goals in directing other human beings.

Ultimate Truth

What is the Way? A place where people walk is called a walkway. A place where cars drive is called a roadway. Thus, there are actual "ways" that have forms and can be recognized. But there are always ways that humans are obliged to practice, which are referred to as ethics and norms. Such norms are abstract, as is the case with social justice, but they exist. Ethics, norms, and social justice are connected with different historical situations and regions. But these norms are also artificial, meaning that they are created by people. Perhaps the most representative form of this are the Confucian ethics of benevolence (*ren*), righteousness (*yi*), propriety (*li*), wisdom (*zhi*), and sincerity (*xin*). It is through these artificial notions that we judge people and weigh the soundness of a society. This artificiality is understood in terms of people's perceptions.

The providence of nature is slightly different, however. In the springtime, it is warm and energy runs through plants to form the first faint buds of green leaves. In the summer, the environment becomes lush, while in the autumn the leaves fall and conceal themselves somewhere out of sight for the winter. Humans experience constant change as well. Societies can also be seen transforming in some direction or another. There is something that exists to cause these changes, and that thing is what we call "principles." There is also an entity that stages these natural phenomena, something that constantly presents itself in new forms according to a certain law. There is a truth that is unseen to our eyes, unheard, such that all things are born, age, sicken, and die according to its principles. That truth is something deep, broad, great, and eternal, something that cannot be understood through the ordinary perceptual abilities or thoughts of humans.

As products of human thinking, ethics and morals exist as a framework with fixed content. We use the word "conservative" to describe adherence to these values and standards—in other words, to the "old." We call it "progressive" when people seek new values and standards with changes in the times. Society is where such ideas exist in widespread conflict, and these ideas and philosophies are ultimately created by people, and they can therefore be understood and named.* The truth, however, is different. It is an absolute entity that cannot be named, something mysterious and multifarious whose content cannot be contained with any name created through human thought.

Because artificial morals are created by human beings, we can understand their concepts and assign them appropriate names. But the specific object of the nonacting truth that characterizes nature eludes the grasp of a person who has not awakened to and unified with it; even when it is said to have been grasped, we understand only part of it, and we understand it wrongly. Its true form is one absolute without subject or object, and when we generate discriminations and pronounce it to be "this thing," we have already lost sight of the true ultimate form of that truth. Thus the Way that we claim to have understood to be "the Way" cannot be the truth of nonaction.

Awakened sages throughout the years have made the utmost sincere efforts to grasp the truth, which they have pronounced to be some form of "Way" or referred to as "nature." Confucius called it by the name of *tian*, or "heaven." Jesus called it by the name of God. The Buddha called it the Dharmakāya Buddha, and Founding Master Sotaesan, the founder of *Won*-Buddhism, used the expression "*Il-Won.*"

The names given centered on the image of this true form captured through the lens of these sages' realization. Many enlightened ones would emerge later and give it new names. Any name given to the truth is ultimately only a substitute; it cannot be said to be its true form. Names to express the truth express only part of its true form, and such names are inevitably expressed.

Ground and Functioning of the Truth

One aspect of how the truth functions is that it is radiant and generates creative transformations, with a component of substance and nature forming its basis. While there is a perspective from which heaven and earth appear to be quietly sleeping, there is also a functioning aspect in which all things appear to be actively operating. It is similar to the way our minds have a very tranquil state without any thoughts at all, yet also have times when they are engaging in this or that manner of thinking.

In the *Daodejing*, the truth is said to be "nameless"** because the aspect that belongs to the truth's substance and nature cannot be estimated with thought nor explained with words. This is said to be the origin of heaven and earth, while the aspect of the truth's functioning is explained as the matrix of all things.

To borrow an expression from Confucianism, this unnameable ground of the truth is called *wuji*, or "ultimate of nonbeing." In the language of *Won*-Buddhism, it is called "true voidness." In the language of Buddhism, it is called "nothingness" or "the void." That which has a name represents the functioning of creation that generates inexhaustible creative transformations upon that nameless ground; this may be called the principle of yin and yang or the law of cause and effect. It may be that this providence was described as a matrix because it presides over the destinies of all things.

How to Understand the Truth

I have already given an explanation regarding the namelessness of substances and nature and the names of functioning. The question we run into now is how to proceed with awakening to this truth. The nameless truth can only be felt and understood by making the mind extremely tranquil and complete. Just as the waves must be calmed before we can see the bottom of the water, so it is true that the realization of extremely subtle truth can only be tasted from a state without ideas and thoughts. With the ultimate Way, realization is only possible when we carry questions with faith and profound attention, immersing ourselves in deep meditation with the utmost sincerity to answer these questions.

The next principle—that of things with names—is always accompanied by desires, by states of mind, and is perceived through activities of thought, such as seeing, hearing, and thinking. The nameless truth that is realized with non-desire can be obtained through practice to unify with the substance and nature that represents oneness of the whole, namely the truth's resting aspect. However, practice with the principle of things with names, which are understood to be accompanied by desires, can be described as a process of understanding the truth's acting aspect, or its parts and phenomena of change. It should be noted, however, that these two types of practice must be carried out in tandem, and it is impossible to state that either one of them is superior.

The Gateway for Releasing and Gathering All Things

Both the profound ground of truth that is described as nameless and the functionings of the Way that are described as having names represent the two sides of an entity's action and rest, its inside and outside, its essence and function. It is like when we speak of houses: we often think only of whether the house itself is good or bad, yet we cannot also ignore the foundation upon which it stands.

That one great truth in which the unchanging nameless Way and the changing principles with names are not divided is like a gateway to a storehouse for bringing in all the world's principles and inexhaustible treasures.

This means that the principles referred to in science and all of its different physical phenomena, such as the principle of heavy things traveling downward, the law of air circulation, or the laws governing the intersection of cold and warm currents, all have their origins in the Way. The doctrines of the many religions come from sages who were awakened to the Way that is the true form of the universe, and extracted from that truth the necessary parts for human life.

*named: These represent another step forward, existing as principles and creative transformations manifested on the ground of the Way. Through them, it is possible to conceptualize and perceive the principles and transformation contrary to the unnameable substance and nature through human reason, and so it is said that we are able to name them.
**nameless: Refers to the substance and nature of the Way or truth. The substance and nature are described as nameless because they cannot be named as any one thing.

Become a Great Liberated Mind

When we think that a beautiful thing is beautiful,
Its opposite, the ugly, has already come into being.
When we perceive the wholesome as being wholesome,
That which is unwholesome is already there.

Thus in natural phenomena
The existing and nonexisting are derived from each other.
The easy and the difficult bring each other into being.
The long and the short are mutually formed.
The high and the low lean on each other

The sound of instruments and the voice are joined.
The front and back follow one another.

But
The sage leaves behind the relative world,
Working with the mind that is absolutely one,
Teaching with actions, not with words,
Edifying living creatures yet shunning honors,
Caring for the people yet acting with no obstruction in the mind,
Teaching with utmost sincerity yet never boasting,
Accumulating achievements yet never lingering.

Oh!
Mere transcendence of the relative world,
Its name is eternal.

When we observe or hear things and we feel them to be beautiful or think them nice, or when we find them foul or evil, there arises in our mind a standard of beauty, a benchmark for what is good. Thus, an opposing ugliness arises as a result of our "beauty" standard when we declaring something beautiful. When we say, "That person is nice," there is necessarily a standard for "nice" and "not nice."

We sometimes say, "That person is tall." Within the word there is a standard of how tall someone must be in order to be "tall" or to be "short," and it is by this standard that we think of and judge and speak of people as tall or short. So it is. When we regard something as beautiful, there is already something relatively foul that inevitably arises. The "good" and "bad" and the "beautiful" and "ugly" of human society arise from these standards of the mind. When the standards are high, beauty is rare; when the standards are low, beauty becomes more frequent.

We describe people who practice politics as being "outstanding politicians" or "corrupt politicians" based on what we think they ought to do. The idea that a husband should behave in this or that way and a wife should behave in this or that way gives rise to the thought that someone is a "wise wife" or a "bad husband."

We must submit these standards to examination. The causes of beauty and ugliness or wholesomeness and unwholesomeness derive from the individual's standards and emerge from the values of peoples and cultures. We ordinary people are prone to having false standards, or to being self-centered or wrongly fixated on wholesomeness and unwholesomeness. In service of mistaken standards, we are constantly comparing in a relativistic way, living a painful life as a result.

Moreover, that which is beautiful or ugly or wholesome or unwholesome differs according to each person's standards or according to need. The objects that are viewed as beautiful or ugly also tend to differ, and we find ourselves acting according to fixed ideas. When we are fixated on these ideas of wholesome and unwholesome, we cannot see correctly. Beyond that, our minds are not free, and we become slaves to our fixed ideas. Being unable to see properly or make wise decisions, we bring misfortune upon ourselves.

Take a look at the myriad natural phenomena that lie before us: the existing and non-existing, the mountains and the seas, the sun and the moon, the high and the low, the long and the short, the prospering and the impoverished... With people as with natural phenomena, it is the ordinary person's attitude to live life in a relativistic way—to live as an extension of nature, the shameful life of living as part of nature.

One of my old classmates has become the president of a company, and now I must too. If someone else is a president, then I should be as well. We live the relativistic life in which we adopt our neighbors' way of life as a standard in our mind and strive to meet that standard. Instead, we must live our lives in accordance with our own standards, and we must know how to proactively change the starting point for our standards according to the situation. Unfortunately, we still find ourselves living relativistic, other-oriented lives because we determine the standards for our own lives based on the lives of others and try to meet them, thinking, "This is how others live," "This is how the world is," "This is what people think," or "This is what famous people do." Sages and people of the Way first stroll in a mind-state of absolute non-action* in which they are bound by nothing relativistic, nor even to their own internal standards, proactively performing the historical mission and responsibilities that have been given to them.

Their minds are always the Sŏn mind of nonaction. Rooted in this mind, they focus their efforts on teaching human beings. As much as possible, they try to teach wordlessly through practice, helping others to see and to feel and to understand themselves. At times, they teach in speech or in text; they may also teach with sternness, depending on the situation.

In the life of Confucius, we can see someone who was passionate about teaching and who taught in a way that was perfect for the learner's situation. As such, Confucius would sometimes say, "I should not speak now. Do heaven and earth not create all things without a word?" We are also encouraged to consider the way in which the Buddha and Jesus taught their students with kindness and love.

The life of the sage is one of teaching and working ceaselessly for the world, and of regarding it as one's innate mission to awaken and love humans without hoping for them to understand, threatening them, or boasting.

*nonaction: This refers to the mind-state and abilities that come from reaching the supreme stage through cultivation of the Way. Inwardly, the mind may be described as being at leisure and free, without being bound by the comparing mind, desire, or ideas; outwardly, one may be working, but doing so in a rational, natural way without being artificial, forced, or contrived. This means that the sage practices according to the Way of the universe, just as the truth of the universe proceeded through nonacting nature when nurturing the myriad objects in existence through the four seasons.

How a Sage Conducts Politics

Lead the people away from battle

By not revering only those who are gifted.

Lead the people away from producing the mind of thievery

By not regarding material things as being of value.

Lead the people away from having confused minds

By not showing ambition.

And so

The sage governing a country

Empties people's mind of selfish desires,

Fills people's belly with true energy,

Sets targets low,
And builds a strong framework (drive) for putting this into practice.

In so doing, he or she governs
By always guiding the people
To eliminate unnecessary defilements and idle thoughts,
To shed their desire,

And by preventing clever intellectuals
From daring to bewilder the public's minds.

In this way,
As he or she governs through reason and nature
There will be not no government.

We must not excessively respect famous people or members of the ruling class or allow our interests to skew toward them. The fear is that when we place too much importance on elites, they will each try to become the ruling class and various forms of balance will be upset.

In Korea, society once centered on members of the Korea Military Academy, and people from particular regions were the ruling class, causing all sorts of trouble. What we call the ruling class must constantly be cycling and free of stagnation so that such a group is never able to monopolize power.

When a society pursues material values excessively, morals and spiritual values collapse and the people become slaves to earthly desires. The phenomena happening today speak clearly to this.

When leaders have too strong a desire for power, they become the object of denunciation by the people, throwing society into disorder and obscuring the standards for educating future generations. The behavior of public figures is tremendously important, and people who burn with a desire for power must not become public figures. A public figure should be someone who is humble and scrupulous in their self-management.

Sages have focused their efforts on edifying the people, but on occasion they have also become political leaders whose goals always lay in edifying the people. When they venture into politics, they deliver their messages—their principles and philosophy—in a very symbolic way. They must always empty their minds of personal interests and selfish desires and focus their efforts on being fair. Otherwise, people are prone to ambition, believing that they will do an excellent job as a government official or succumbing to delusions of grandeur and thinking, "It must be me," or forming bands to hold power permanently and representing the interests of themselves and their followers.

Those who hope to study the political ways of the sages must work diligently to empty their minds. Yet emptying one's mind is not enough; that empty mind-ground should be filled with a true spirit of love for one's country, of edifying its people, and of making its economy strong.

Korean politician Kim Koo once said, "The first thing is independence for Korea, and the second, third, and fourth things are also independence for Korea." In these words, one can sense his true energy, his suffusion with patriotic feeling. Like the kind and loving mind of India's Mahatma Gandhi, who forgave the man who shot him, we must fill ourselves with a mind of love for human beings.

When governing a country or managing an organization, one must set standards that are low enough to give a sense of comfort to the ordinary members of the working class who are following along. One must work to ensure that everyone can share in the pleasure of achieving goals.

That driving force must also be made strong, so that people are given the courage and drive to accomplish the goal. If the framework of a pursuit is weak, society as a whole may succumb to defeatism, resulting in diminished morale that leaves it in a state where it cannot accomplish anything at all.

Laozi presented the people of China with the high educational ideal of being "without knowledge and without desire." His message was that each individual citizen had to have a mind without knowledge and without desire in order to have a life truly replete with the essential original mind of a human being. Typically, we seek to possess quantitatively large amounts of things, yet when we fixate on quantity, we become slaves to desire. It is only when we guide all people to be possessors of the true Sŏn mind, I think, that we can ultimately promote the overall quality of life to its highest level. Laozi foresees a grand plan for turning all people into cultivators of the Way—in other words, making them true people.

He also saw a major reason for social disorder was misleading values stemming from intellectuals who lacked a spirit of ownership; he located the responsibility for that chaos in the class guiding public opinion. An important task of the person practicing governance, he believed, was to ensure that their minds were truly the minds of owners who loved their country and its people, and to prevent the public from being influenced by mistaken information or criticism.

The Truth Has No Origin

The utter emptiness of the truth
Works in all things yet seems to not exist.
The profoundness of the truth
Is like the head of all things.

The truth can pare down the sharp,
Neatly arrange the disordered,
Tame the brilliant into mildness,
Existing together with all things
Down to the smallest speck of dust.

Clear, utterly clear,
The truth exists, seeming both to exist and to not.

I do not know either
Whose child the truth is.
Perhaps it even came before the Supreme Emperor.

The Way described by Laozi has no face. It has no form. It makes no sound. It cannot be touched, seen, or heard. For this reason, he calls it "empty." But it is not nonexistent; the truth clearly exists. It cannot be fully expressed in words, nor can it be conceived as "this" or "that" by the mind. Thus, we may call it an "entity of nothingness." It is because the truth is an entity of nothingness that it transcends all things. It does not fixate on all things, and for this reason is capable of fairness. Thus the functionings of the truth are transcendent functionings, creative transformations without obstruction by selfish desires. The truth is the most fundamental origin. It is the deepest truth and the source. It is the origin that produces the very first beginning. We may therefore say that it forms the origin for all things.

Our attention is often directed at merely phenomenal matters. Our interests are often focused on the development of civilization—the clothes, food, shelter, and culture we need to survive—and on seeking convenience. But if we are to cultivate a life of the truth by going beyond our material and physical life, we must also have a profound interest in the unknowable truth and Way that enable phenomena to be phenomena.

A state exerts its power by constantly doing work for its people. Just as a state exerts great influence on the lives of its people by presenting them with various policies, programs, and goals, so the truth uses its power and creative transformations to unceasingly transform the myriad phenomena. By looking at a few examples of this, we can see that when objects reach an extreme level of prosperity, the truth will break them. Just as a winter that is too cold will be slowly calmed and its wintry energy weakened, any part of the state that grows too much will undergo a slow decline. All things are adjusted so that once they reach an extreme they can no longer be excessive.

Look at how plants flourish during the summer. If the growth becomes too disorderly or is neglected, it is tended to and made orderly again, sometimes through the arrival of fall; disorder in a society brings strictness. When children become too noisy in school, one of them will shout for everyone to be quiet, thus establishing order. Things that shine too brightly become darkened. Minds that are too clear and thoughts that are too bright will darken once they reach an extreme. We must rest. This act of balancing also functions so that the darkness of night comes once the light of day has become too much.

The truth exists in every speck of dust, every microbe and insect, and its creative transformations and functions are granted equally and appropriately to all. Those who understand the wondrous functioning of this truth are obliged to live respectfully and humbly, remaining ever cautious of the great power of that functioning of the truth.

For how long has the truth existed? In our consciousness, there exists a logic related to beginnings and endings. The truth has no beginning, nor any end; it is eternal and always existing. Since long ago, we have imagined the thing that governs human society to be a God with absolute omnipotence, envisioning and personifying its eternity and all-powerfulness as an object of respect and worship. Eastern societies have spoken of the "Supreme Emperor" or "Jade Emperor," while Western societies have spoken of an absolute single God. Laozi says that truth is the mother of God, and that the Way is more original, more essential than God.

The Creative Transformations of the Empty Way

The truth, not being bound to any one thing,
Can govern correctly for the properties of all things.
The sage, not being bound by personal feelings,
Teaches according to the characteristics of the person.

The truth is like the space between heaven and earth,
Empty like the inside of the bellows.
It is empty yet never exhausted,
Manifesting creative transformations as it moves.

Where there are many words, there is much defiance of the Way's
principles.
None can match emptying and observing tranquility.

In this excerpt, "heaven and earth" refer to the truth. The truth is
not bound by human feeling and is free from all things. Humans
fixate on the desire to possess and on principal convictions, and
thus cannot make fair and right decisions. Heaven and earth,
however, do not fixate on beauty and ugliness, wholesomeness
and unwholesomeness; they manage all things, killing what must
be killed and saving what must be saved.

The truth does not take anyone's side. The truth responds appropriately to the individual situations of all people and things.
For this reason, it is nonbenevolent—unlike humans, it is not governed by feelings.

Sages too strive to emulate the functionings of the truth, and
so they do not entertain mistaken thoughts or engage in mistaken
actions because they are bound by both closeness and the lack
of closeness. As they are ever free from human and natural environments, this does mean that they treat things carelessly like
straw dogs but that they are not constrained or obstructed and are
therefore free to grant great virtue, great grace, and true love.

The bellows have an empty body; the flute is hollow inside.
The former object is empty, yet we can fill it with air to make a
fire; with the flute, we can produce all sorts of profound sounds.

In the same way, the truth is empty like the heaven and earth, yet it commands creative transformations of all things. In the first chapter, this was called the "gateway that contains all of the myriad marvelous principles." That empty place of the truth is described as the place where a never-resting grace is produced and a source of creative transformations.

In the text of the "*Il-Won-Sang* Vow" of *Won*-Buddhism, this is described as the "gateway of birth and death that transcends being and nonbeing." This means that the truth produces and gathers all things from a position in which it has transcended all existence and nonexistence, kindness and evil, good and bad, the worthwhile and the worthless.

"The truth has no beginning or end and acts tirelessly on all things." In offering this explanation, Laozi humbly wonders whether or not it is too specific an explanation for the truth. I also wonder if he was not posing a question to himself out of the fear that his students, who had not awakened themselves, might hear this explanation and vainly build up their imagination without knowing for certain.

I think that Laozi himself meant that he ought to take refuge in that empty realm of the truth, that truth realm without discrimination or distracting thoughts and delusions, rather than finding solace in the kind of idea that grows more distant the more we think about it.

Confucius too once told his students, "I am speaking too much. I will not speak now." When one student asked him what he would do if not teach, he answered, "When have heaven and earth ever spoken?"

Sages seem to have the sort of mind that seeks to yearn for and take refuge in the original realm, the thought before the word and the mind before the thought.

The Truth Seems Existing yet Nonexistent

The valley of the empty truth,* divinity
Is eternally without extinction.
It is a mysterious woman.

That mysterious gateway of the woman
Is like the origin that produces all things.

Seeming as though it exists yet does not exist, it constantly enables
   existence.
When using it, we must be idle.

"Valley" refers to the empty space between one mountain and another. "Divinity" is a word used to describe radiance, light, and creative transformations. It is a term to describe the Way that harbors wisdom and capabilities on an empty ground. The truth cannot be described in words, and yet inexhaustible power of creative transformation flows from it.

It is the place within the cow in which the calf is produced. While we cannot say whether there is something contained within the truth as there is within the cow, this explanation offers the cow as a comparison to the truth because of how mysteriously the calf seems to come from it.

He writes that the truth itself is "as though it exists" because it would be inappropriate to say that it clearly does exist. Since those long ago days, we have explained it by saying that it is "that which seems existing yet nonexistent, nonexistent yet existing." When an object has form, it is clear that if it exists it exists, and if it does not exist it does not. The absolute entity exists ambiguously, such that it is not captured by our senses, yet its functioning is without limit or end. When human beings act, they must rest at some point from their hard work. There is a remittance for our love. We should reflect on this comparison between the functioning of the truth and the artificial actions of the human being.

A person engaged in mind-practice—in other words, cultivating the Way—should have some standard for his or her cultivation after reading this chapter.

If we observe our minds, we can see that there is clearly a mind that is ours. The things we like, the things we dislike, the things we loathe, the things we love, and the impressions engraved deeply on our hearts are all clear to see. But what is the mind-ground that bears the weight of these clearly visible thoughts?

If we look at the ground, we find countless seeds embedded in it. When the time is right, they begin to sprout. In the same way, the mind-seeds have clear feelings of favor and disfavor, yet their ground remains unknowable. This mind-ground is the mind that seems to be both existent and nonexistent. We call this "no mind," or "true voidness." When we go through our days preserving this mind and not losing it, caring for it as we would something truly important, this is called the "Sŏn mind" or the "Way mind." Finding and keeping this mind is ultimate bliss and paradise.

Here, we accumulate deep cultivation with preserving the original, empty, and tranquil mind that is our valley divinity. Because the valley divinity seems both existent and nonexistent, we must continue nurturing the nature of it constantly like a spinning thread without killing it with desire or allowing ourselves to become slaves to thoughts or ideas that would otherwise obscure it.

Those who cultivate the Way must commit their sincerest efforts to constantly observing and protecting their original mind, for it is by how much we preserve that original mind that profound wisdom and capability arise. Yet as we encounter objects and act frequently upon them, the mind of preservation becomes diminished and damaged accordingly. For this reason, we are told to work diligently to avoid such situations.

A great practitioner of the Way, then, strives to preserve that original mind without producing minds in response to small things, without involving him- or herself in unnecessary affairs, and without frequent action.

*Valley of the empty truth: The valley of divinity; another name for the Way. It refers to the emptiness of the valley and mysterious nature: the truth is empty, yet it is not fully empty, something living yet empty that harbors mystery within.

The Sage Achieves the Great Self

Heaven and earth are eternal.

How can they enjoy eternal life?

It is because there is no mind to preserve themselves.

Thus, heaven and earth are eternal.

Because the sage emulates heaven and earth,

Setting aside his or her own interests,

He or she is in fact before others,

Serving without tending to him- or herself,

And his or her name shines eternally.

Is this not purely forsaking selfish desires?

So does the sage accomplish the great self.

The sage has no selfish desires.

The process by which a person achieves growth with him- or herself depends on what his or her ideal in life is, what model he or she adopts. Those who model themselves on unexceptional friends or neighbors, those model themselves on knowledge, those who model themselves on well-mannered people... the ordinary person lives as though he or she has no one to emulate. It is very important, then, for the development of character that we have something to emulate, something to which we can compare ourselves constantly over the course of our growth.

When we are students, we have textbooks. Once we leave school, though, the textbooks gradually disappear, and we do not have textbooks for life as we face real-world problems.

It goes without saying that the best textbooks are the scriptures of the sages. Yet what are the textbooks used by the sages themselves? The answer is the truth, the principles, heaven and earth, and nature. We do not know how to make the principles of the universe our textbooks, much less heaven and earth and nature. Laozi also regarded principles as his textbook, and in this section he describes how we knew to adopt heaven and earth and nature as his textbook.

The nature that is heaven and earth merely exists as it is, without states of mind and without a sense of self-esteem without attempting to present itself well, keep itself long in existence, or reject the unclean. Thus it has existed for eternal *kalpa* (eons) without being worn out or hindered by anyone.

We humans have minds that fixate to an extreme degree on ourselves. Thus we cause ourselves to suffer and others hinder and malign us, preventing us from preserving what honor and forms we have. Naive children do not have the discrimination to seek food for themselves, and so many gather around them to help and support them as they grow.

We often speak of people falling into their own traps. The person who tries to construct him- or herself in some particular way can never enjoy true happiness. We must truly study the mindless simpleness of heaven and earth so that we can live easily and comfortably.

The modern person is excessively self-conscious. Because of this self-consciousness, we compare ourselves to others, trying to change ourselves in one way or another; our comparisons show us to be lesser than those next to us, and because we are lesser we suffer. Because we suffer, we develop negative thoughts toward life rather than positive ones. Many social problems arise as a result.

We are always going through our lives comparing ourselves to others and competing. If those rivals disappear, we create new rivals. In the process, we are followed by those worse off than us, and we follow those who seem better off than us. This life of pursuing and being pursued occurs because we are too conscious of ourselves. We can only achieve great success and live absolutely when we tear down this self-consciousness and live as the great self and the forgotten self.

Let Us Go through Life like Water

The truly great things
Are like water.

Water brings benefits to all things
Yet it fights not for its place.
It dwells in the places that the people despise.
Is it not thus like the truth?

Sages, like water,
Wish for the lowest stations.

They use their minds deeply
And are benevolent with others.
They speak reliably;
They govern effectively;
They handle their work consummately.
When they act, they always choose the right action for the occasion.

This is how the sages use their minds without the comparing mind,
Thus they are without flaws.

In Laozi's view, the most outstanding textbook among all the myriad objects is water. Water is the source of life, and it offers all sorts of benefits to all things, most notably when it washes away filth. It also does not compete, and in its willingness to lie in the low places that humans all despise, it is similar to the functioning of the truth.

The truth feeds and sustains all things; it does not distinguish between dirty and clean but embraces all things and does not forsake them. At the same time, it is a hidden truth that does not brag about itself. It is in this way that water is described as comparable to the truth. Yet he recounts how the actions of the sages, perhaps because they have long modeled themselves on this truth, have shown similarities to the actions of water.

In contrast to ordinary people, sages behave humbly when in low places. The outlays of their minds are extremely deep, they behave with love in their interactions with people, and they are cautious and exhibit control with their words, which must be words that can be put into practice. They govern people effectively, and when they move, they make sure that it suits the situation. When we handle our affairs, it is extremely important that we move in a way that is perfectly suited to the situation.

The sage also has no state of mind relating to competition with other people. When another seeks to go ahead, the sage yields and lowers him- or herself so that the other can go ahead. Because he or she has no state of mind relating to competition, his or her own mind is calm and at ease.

In Buddhism, the world of the ideal mind is called "samadhi without conflict." This refers to a state of mind in which urges relating to competition and comparison come to rest, when the mind of comparison and distinguishing between "superior" and "inferior" comes to rest. This state is truly the ultimate bliss and the Sŏn mind.

Because they have no state of mind relating to competition, they are not subject to hatred or hindrance from others. Thus, we can achieve peace and comfort whenever we are in their presence.

Once You Have Achieved Merits, Step Back

Filling oneself with possessing all things
Is not better than being loose and wanting.
The sharpness of wisdom,
One cannot guard that edge deeply.

The richness of material things,
One cannot keep it eternally.
Being wealthy and arrogant,
One cannot shake away faults.

When you make your name by achieving things,
Quickly back away from that post;
This is the truthful life.

When you seek too many honors and powers, can you hope to hold on to them? The principle stands that when something is excessive, it will necessarily collapse. You must stop when you think that something is suitable for you. If you do not stop, the truth will take it away. If you act first to give it to others before it is taken away, it will become an accumulation of virtue and come back to you. But once it has been taken away, it will not come back, and your honor will be tarnished. Consider the greed of politicians. The question, then, is when it is time to give something up, when it is time to quit. The answer is that you should quit when you want it a bit more. That is the most suitable moment.

When people who routinely criticize based on their wisdom and knowledge always possess honors and powers, it demands a truly large amount of time and mental energy to hold on to these honors and powers. Do honors, powers, and the like truly hold enough meaning to be preserved at the expense of so many other things? We ought to think carefully about this.

In benefitting our own lives, it is more worthwhile to have the leisure of preserving our original nature, to have stability of the mind, rather than striving to hold on to outside things (honors and powers). It seems better for outward honors and powers to be loose enough that they are not difficult for us to cope with. Even if a time inevitably comes when we are told that for the sake of society or the state we shall be entrusted with honors or powers, it is wise to avoid staying that way for too long.

Even the masters of all the different fields cannot always show the sharpest of foresight. They become lethargic or complacent, or they collapse due to the efforts of others rather than themselves. We must know to stop before we collapse, or we should do our best to live with a humble mind and not fixate on winning first place.

If we have achieved success and been recognized for it, we should not forget to have the humility of spirit to share our success with others, to decline praise, and to step back.

There is no more dangerous a time than when we have become the top person in our field and our honors are at their highest. Ordinary people, however, merely rejoice in happiness when their achievements are most recognized, only to suddenly find themselves shivering in the chill of dishonor.

Observe the Master

Can we become one with the truth in using the spirit
In such a way that we are able to not leave the original nature?

Can we devote to energy with the utmost softness
Until ours is like the softness of a newborn?

Can we polish and polish the mind to utmost clarity
And make it without the smallest speck?

Can we love the people and govern the country

With the empty mind?

Can we open and close the mind's gate at will
And be like the woman?

When mastering affairs and principles
Can we ably hide our knowledge?

Though we bear and raise people,
We do not place them in our minds.
Though we achieve things in our work, we do not boast.
Becoming the best, we do not interfere in all things.
This is said to be the consummation of truthful virtue.

The term "using the spirit" refers to the functioning of the spirit. It is a question posed to the person at an advanced level of cultivation of the Way: "Are you capable of spiritual functioning without leaving the original nature?" The sage who exists at a high level has awakened to the truth of the universe and models him- or herself on that truth by disciplining his or her spirit. The most fundamental aspect of disciplining the spirit is unifying with the original nature that is the foundation of one's own mind—what is communicated with the word "Way." Our life is a continuation of the functioning of the spirit, and it is a truly difficult form of cultivation for us to never leave that realm of the original nature when using that functioning spirit that burns so intensely. A person who is familiar with mind-practice is said never to leave the self-nature, and we must question whether ours has become the kind of practice that allows for this.

The term "devote to energy" refers to the practitioner of the Way's perfect discipline regarding energy and emotions. Human beings live their lives using energy internally. When we use that energy without having engaged in discipline or practice, it becomes coarse, or we are unable to achieve stability, or it becomes scattered, or we behave violently. The practitioner of the Way, however, always regards this disciplined use of energy as practice to modulate his or her feelings. He or she always puts this into practice so that his or her energy is under the spirit's control and his or her loving attitude is achieved very peacefully and softly in the ultimate stage.

In cultivation, the practitioner of the Way sets the goal of pure and clear one-pointedness, the mind that is unsullied by grime. Internally, the ordinary human is filled with desires, defilements, and distracting thoughts. As a result, there are constantly arising states of joy and anger, sorrow and happiness, and we live lives of suffering. The sage who has achieved a considerable amount of mind-practice knows how to shake away the dust that is eating away at the mind. We also learn how to open and close the doors of our own mind by cultivating the Way. The ordinary person does not recognize his or her own states; being unaware, he or she does not know how to close the door of the mind, nor how to open it. Instead, he or she lives life as it comes.

A house has a door. When guests come and knock on the door, someone will open it if a good person is there, and if a bad person comes that same person will close the door tightly. The family members inside will open and close the door when they go in or out of the house. In this way, the door plays an important role in ensuring the peace of the family. In the same way, it is of truly great importance to know how to open and close the doorway of our mind.

When we become a politician who governs a state or when we are training a student, and we do so with a mind geared toward ambition or honor, the governing will be unnatural; it will center on ourselves as a politician and we will rule by force or by violence.

It is through this process that the public comes to suffer hardship as a result of its political leaders. This also means that a sage in power will take the side of the public, governing properly and naturally as the country's circumstances dictate.

By cultivating the Way, we ultimately gain freedom of the mind and peace and we acquire wisdom. We achieve a wisdom born not of knowledge but of having awakened to the truth. What we are asked here, however, is whether, once we have acquired this wisdom, we have the self-control to use it only where it should be used with humility, to manage that wisdom effectively. The unwise person with knowledge carries that knowledge like a tool for living or boasts of that knowledge to others, so that the knowledge becomes a rope ensnaring him or her, a blade that divides society. We must therefore have the self-control to know when to use true wisdom where its use is needed and to hide its light in places where it ought not to be used.

The question is whether we have become someone truly capable of granting love, someone who does not boast of teaching and helping others succeed, who does not boast or interfere excessively in the works of those beneath him or her as an important person in charge, and who is not swept away by arrogant notions by giving oneself credit. Those who pride themselves on having done a bit of mind-practice should read this section and sense the fearsome warning that it contains.

Beneficial Because It Is Empty

The thirty spokes of the cart wheel

Converge on a single hub;

Because that hub is empty,

We are finally able to use it as a cart.

When we sculpt mud and burn the vessel

The vessel is hollow inside,

Thus we can use it as a vessel.

When we use doors and windows to create a room,

It serves as a room because it is empty inside.

Thus the benefit of the things that exist
Lies in making use of their emptiness.

The previous sections have taught that the truth, or the Way, is like an empty space within an empty valley. The sage who is proficient at cultivating the Way has awakened to this nameless truth and attempts to use it actively in perfecting his or her character.

From observing objects in the real world, we can see that vessels, cart wheels, and rooms can be used to our benefit because they are empty inside. This is not true only of the myriad objects of the world: how exasperating it is to find when we use the mind that it is filled with prejudice, filled with states of mind relating to hate toward others, filled with states of mind that favor others, filled with one or another goal, filled with the idea that one's own methods are supreme! Only when we clean our minds well and boldly rid them of the fixed notions that fill them does true freedom arise and creative ability begin to flow forth.

The truth, too, is empty, and so there may arise the creative transformations to fairly minister to all things without exception. The sage's mind is also empty, and so wisdom and courage and loving-kindness may flow from it.

The blackboards that we find in schools are used in various ways, yet they must be cleaned with an eraser before they are fully available for the next use. So it is with the functioning of our minds: our minds' workings are innumerable, yet if we do not erase them, we cannot use them again with vitality. So it is that the modern person lives amid torment of the mind, feeling severe division, depression, and delusional phenomena of the mind. To heal this suffering in our mind, we must wash our minds as we wash our faces; we must take to heart that the mind should be emptied clean before we can rejoice in using it powerfully with a spirit of creation.

Spiritual Pleasure

Our eyes blur because of the five colors.
Our ears are deafened because of the five sounds.
Our appetite is spoiled because of the five tastes.

To ride a horse across the fields and mountains
Exhilarates the mind.
When we make possible things that are difficult to attain
Our behavior naturally wanders.

Sages grasp

Not that which is visible outside
But the substance within.

Humans live through senses that have developed into habit. Once tainted by artificial senses, we lose the sounds and flavors and feeling of pure nature. The closer these artificial sounds and flavors and colors come to nature, the more peaceful and purer they become. The farther our senses are from nature, the more deeply the sickness resides. Nature is great. If we work diligently to return to nature, our diseases will be cured by it.

In the distant past, people rode horses when they hunted. Today, we race about using the modern convenience of automobiles. The mind falls prey to giddiness. When the mind is giddy, we begin to rove, to hover. It seems appropriate, then, to describe modern people as those who have "lost their homes." They have lost the hometown of their mind, their original nature, and so they are fated to suffer. Living in an environment where giddiness is inevitable, we must commit a truly great amount of time to the practice of calming the mind.

We use our minds countless times over the course of a day. In what we call our "information society," we must produce many thoughts to adapt to all the noises and the media, the complex structure. It is because of that we cannot get our minds under control.

Surely there are many people who have found themselves in

a state where the functioning of their mind is out of control, like a car with broken brakes. What efforts are we making to cause those divisions and delusions to subside? It is truly something fearsome. We must begin practicing to calm this mind.

When we have great riches, we find ourselves wanting to boast and to possess more. Ultimately, it is not people who own riches but the opposite: it is the riches that come to own people.

As a result, our characters collapse, leaving only these riches while condemning us to live a dissolute life. The important thing is not whether we have riches or not; the problem is that humans are consumed by riches.

The attitude of sages toward life is not the pursuit of a sensory life of showing off to others but the pursuit of a life of absolute value that is faithful to one's self-nature. Typically, people are seduced by the beauty of flowers and forget the genuineness of bearing fruit. The flower is but a preparatory stage for the formation of fruit. Instead of being seduced by beautiful flowers, we must focus our attention on the genuine fruit.

Favor and Humiliation

Whether it be favor that comes or humiliation,
Act with the same caution and gather your spirit.
Even if great hardship visits,
Regard that hardship as being as precious as your own body.

Why do I say to come to your senses before favor and humiliation?
Because we often fall because of favor.
We must be careful in accepting favor should we obtain it.
We must collect our senses should we lose favor.
This is why we should collect our senses as though amazed at

favor or humiliation.

Why do I say to regard great hardship as being as precious as our
   own bodies?
When great hardship comes upon me
It is enough for me to take responsibility for that hardship.
Were I someone who could not cope with hardship,
What great hardship would come my way?

And so
The person who regards the world as being as precious as his or
   her body
Is capable of asking favor from heaven and earth.
The person who loves heaven and earth as he or she loves his or
   her body
May be entrusted with the salvation of heaven and earth.

When honors come to us, when we acquire authority or are recognized by those higher than us, there arises a problem. We become self-satisfied and disregard others or neglect ourselves. When we are arrogant, we lose people. When we are lazy, we hinder improvement. When power and favor come to the wise person, he or she considers his or her own capabilities. The wise person knows how to decline excessive honors that do not suit his or her capabilities; where they are appropriate, he or she accepts them cautiously while striving not to suffer any damage to his or her humanity from those honors or lose sight of his or her own duty.

When humiliations come, in contrast, we should not respond with thoughtless anger or rebellion. Instead, we should think quietly. If there is some cause behind it that we must endure, then we should know to repent, to submit humbly and accept the corresponding punishment. Yet even when humiliations are incomprehensible, we should look at the conditions with equanimity and commit ourselves to extricating ourselves with equanimity. In such cases when it cannot be avoided, we should understand it to be the visitation of transgressive karma created in a former life, which requires the heedfulness to love our fate with equanimity. When we strive amid humiliation without resigning ourselves or losing our hopes for the distant future, we are sure to escape it eventually, and it is actually through these humiliations that we hone our wisdom and capabilities.

When faced with great hardships that cannot be overcome easily, we focus on avoiding them, or we resent others. Yet there are times for focusing all our efforts on boldly accepting and overcoming them; when the truth is in the process of creating great people, its first act is to test them. People, too, must pass various tests in their lives to become wise. The person who takes on great responsibilities is tested with great hardships; those who overcome adverse circumstances are entrusted with great things, while those who avoid them or are thwarted by them will find great responsibility slipping farther into the distance.

It is said that the times make the person. The message is that when we are faced with adverse circumstances or the nation is faced with disaster, there will emerge a national leader who will undertake various efforts to overcome this hardship.

We must understand that great people grow amid problems and crises and hardships and have the courage and wisdom to know how to value adverse circumstances and overcome them.

The Truth Has No Face

The form of the truth
Is called "plain," for it has no color.
The sound of the truth
Is called "rare," for it cannot be heard.
The body of the truth
Cannot be grasped,
And so we call it "slight," for it is very slender.
With these three characteristics, the truth
Cannot be fully illuminated;
It is one, mixed.

Though it is high up, it is not bright;
Though it is down low, it is not dark.
It continues without stopping yet it cannot be named.

Returning ultimately to nothing,
It is the form without form;
It is the form without division,
Yet it is something rapturous.
In general, this truth is such that,
Though we look up, we cannot see its head;
Though we chase it, we cannot find its tail.

Taking the morals illuminated long ago
And applying them to this day
Is to awaken to the origins of the truth
And take them as the bearings for our actions.

The original essence of the truth, we are told, is the sort of entity that cannot be grasped with our human senses. This was described in the first chapter as the "truth without a name," yet the explanation in this chapter was sensory. It is described as the colorless thing that we cannot see when we seek to view it with our eyes, the faint thing that we cannot hear when we seek to hear it, the entity of nothingness so delicate that it cannot be grasped when we seek to hold it in our hands.

No one has seen God, who is described as an absolute entity in the universe and the creator of all things. If someone claims to have seen God, it is a misapprehension; that was not God. So let us instead seek this aspect of the truth within our minds. The times when we are best capable of understanding the Way are when our minds are tranquil and empty. Let us describe the mind at that moment as "the Way."

The truth is the sort of entity that cannot be appropriately described as one thing or another, that cannot be fully expressed with human language capabilities. At the same time, it carries within us much grace and radiance and many creative transformations.

In spatial terms, the Way is present equally in all things. When it is somewhere high, and even more so when it is somewhere low and not bright, it is not dark. There is no more light in the mind of the sage, nor does it shine less in the mind of the dull person. The Way also exists continuously through time. It is not something that can be calculated or fathomed in quantitative terms so that we say there is more of the Way at some times and less of the Way at others.

When we try to venerate the Way for its sacredness, we find no separate part that constitutes its head; when we look along it for its tail, we find no end. It is so rapturous an entity that it cannot be described, where everything is head and everything tail, something truly unknowable—more unknowable the more we think about it.

Though the truth is something that cannot be defined as any one thing, it is also a thing that can be seen, heard, grasped, and known, for the practitioner of the Way who commits him- or herself sincerely to their studies and pursuing it may indeed awaken to it.

Since long ago, sages have awakened to the unseen truth that governs and transforms all things in the universe, using it as their standard to share morals (that is, the doctrines of the world's religions). They have taught it so that it would become a norm for society and serve as a guide for people's behavior. If we look within our own minds, we find internal norms that state how people should act. We call this a "conscience." What we call consciousness is in some sense a moral concept, what we must call the moral code presented by all sages of the past. Since long ago, humankind has used this as the basis for ethical promises. This ethical consciousness, the root of the prevailing notions of society, is based in the Way of the universe. The nature of those norms obviously changes between eras and societies, but however much it changes, it bears an absolute relationship with what the sages of the past have awakened to and illuminated, and it is for this reason that it is called the "guide ropes of morality."

People Who Possess the Truth

Because the great scholars of long ago

Mastered the subtle truth,

We cannot fathom what this profound character may be.

In general, it

Cannot be confined

As being this or that kind of person.

We will try to force ourselves to describe its appearance:

Hesitant!

As though crossing over thin ice...

Looking about!

As though searching for fear of what will come from the four
  directions.

Dignified!

Like an invited guest. . .

Easy!

Like ice melting.

Plain! Like an as-yet untouched log. . .

Vast! Like the hollowness of the valley. . .

Chaotic! Like the muddy waters that flow together.

Who can ably make him- or herself as though turbid

Yet can also make that stain gently subside

And make it clear?

Who can ably make him- or herself comfortable,

Gradually taking a sickened world

And striving to bring it back to life?

The person who has made the truth part of him- or herself

Has a mind that is bound by nothing at all.

Possessing the eternal truth,

He or she abandons the new with its many changes.

It is because of the presence of this truth that governs heaven and earth and all things that we have spring, summer, fall, and winter, and all things are governed in a way that is suited to their nature. Sometimes it saves and sometimes it slays; it brings both the warmth of the spring breeze and the chill of the winter wind.

For this reason, the truth cannot be described as any one thing. It gives good things to people and also bad things. Those with the character to awaken to this truth, to discipline their mind and body and make what they have awakened to into their own, can not be described in such limited terms as being "kind," "wise," or "capable." Indeed, such people are difficult to fathom, even.

Ordinary people live lives of desire, and so a few experiences with them are enough that we can assess them as "kind," "educated," or "good at their work." The person who adopts the truth as a standard for his or her mind-practice has such a great variety of aspects that Confucius was led to say, "The superior person is not a limited vessel."

If we look at the dharma instructions, the sages are shown to be free, to show both capability and pettiness, to treat others with brightness and to appear inarticulate, to give the appearance of fixating on affairs while also letting go of affairs and achieving liberation.

The original truth is great and empty. The minds of sages are thus untainted by greed, unbound by ideas or signs, by doctrines or arguments. The sage is one who understands how to preserve this empty truth. The great and empty truth is something eternal, without beginning or end. The sage who travels together with that eternal truth does not fixate on new things or all these things' transformations.

This chapter remarks briefly on the external qualities of the sage and the master of the Way. As noted before, however, the sage's character is highly mutable and cannot be defined in limited terms.

The next aspect is carrying ideas into action with the greatest of care. It is the sort of caution in which we always consider our own capabilities and circumstances and consider the situation carefully, adapting to those conditions before making a decision and saying, "This appears to be the optimal way of doing things." When we are unaware of this, we proceed boldly, declaring things to be this way or that. The person who is proficient at it may be well aware, yet must also show great consideration and caution, for new variables must be taken into deep consideration when transforming such things into reality.

Such people are also unquestionably dignified, with such a bearing to them that others cannot simply speak of them with disregard. Indeed, we have people around us that we cannot treat casually. They are people possessed of deep consideration, bold determination, and the power of consistent practice, people with a sacred spiritual capability.

Yet another aspect is the ability to insist on something and show a great degree of fixation, but to concede very simply on all things once they have changed their mind. To me it seems that this capability exists because they are training themselves throughout life with a mind-nature of liberation and freedom that is not chained to any one place.

Simplicity is said to resemble the tree stump that has never been pruned. It denotes an approach that is free of artifice. We pretend to know, fancy ourselves successful, fancy ourselves superior, make ourselves up, and so we are false and lack simplicity. The sage has the purity to do what he or she can do and not do what he or she cannot.

The section mentioned effortless capability. When confronted with an unclean social environment, the sage is possessed of the unseen ability to appear turbid without being turbid, to exist in turbid places and slowly, without anyone's knowledge, to replace these foul things with an atmosphere of cleanliness.

The sage's mind is at ease in the face of a sickened world and a morally debased society, yet the sage has the hidden ability to cure each of those diseases of society without others knowing. This power is a power that comes from awakening to and disciplining themselves with the truth. The difference between the abilities of ordinary humans and sentient beings and those of sages could be said to lie in whether those abilities are possessed of the truth.

All Things Return to Their Roots

When the empty mind
Reaches the extreme
And the tranquil mind
Is closely guarded,

Though all things
Emerge together,
I may know
To where they return.

In general, all things
Ceaselessly function
Yet all of them follow
Their roots.

Returning to the original truth
We are tranquil.
Being tranquil
We return to the self-nature;
Recovering the realm of the self-nature
We unite with the ultimate truth.

Knowing the truth,
We will say it is bright.
Not knowing the truth,
Childishly,
We commit unspeakable acts.

Knowing the truth,
We accept the clean and the turbid;
When our vision is broad
We will be fair;
Being fair
We will be the greatest;
Being the greatest,
Is one not a sage?

When we become people of heaven
We will illuminate morals then and there.
The sage's word is eternal.
When we accept and practice these morals
There will never be any danger.

Once practitioners of the Way awaken to the truth, they focus sincerely on making it part of themselves, practicing with particular thoroughness to achieve tranquility of the mind. So when they are capable of returning to their tranquil nature and preserving it at all times and places, they can understand clearly the movements of the transformations in all things in the world and the fact that those transformations necessarily follow principles.

When we return to the original ground of the truth and the mind is extremely tranquil, we unify with the nameless Way, and when we attain that tranquility, radiant wisdom will inevitably flow forth. When we achieve wisdom, we establish the ground to grasp the sequence and circumstances of rise and fall, prosperity and degeneration in human affairs and make proper decisions, becoming a pioneer and leader in society.

Because we understand the fundamental principles of the filthy and simple aspects of reality, the simple within the filthy, and the transformation of the simple into the filthy, there arises the great capacity to accept both the pure and the sullied.

When we accept both the pure and the sullied, our ability to see objects expands and we can therefore make fair decisions. When we are fair and impartial, we can become a leader in our organization. When we understand this truth and become a leader, we can establish order in our society and guide human beings properly.

How can a leader be wise, how can he or she show a fundamental acceptance, how can he or she apply a truly balanced attitude of fairness in real life when he or she fails to understand the truth?

When one awakens to the truth and uses that wisdom to observe human society and the things to come in the future, the one speaks appropriate words (doctrines), and those words gradually become the prevailing ideas spoken of by people in society, the standards for living, and the benchmarks of conscience. Such a person is said to be a sage.

What methods exist to help humans escape from suffering? There is no other way but to awaken to the truth and become a sage. What is the human's path away from greed? We appeal to our conscience, crying, "Get rid of it! Get rid of it!" Yet there is no other path that will allow us to eliminate or control greed. We must realize that there is no way but to become a sage by awakening to and practicing the truth.

Politics of Faith

In the best-governed politics
The public underneath
Knows only that there is a ruler;

After that,
The ruler loves the people,
Governing with their admiration;

After that,
He or she governs the people

So that they are fearful;

After that, he or she governs the people disgracefully.

Thus, when faith is lacking in governance,
Even one who does well is not trusted.
Be careful!
Regard your promises as exceedingly precious.
When great things are achieved and one succeeds,
May your politics be those of rejoicing
That the people all say they have done well.

The most extraordinary form of politics is the kind of governance by which the nameless truth creates, transforms, and nurtures all things, without our even being aware that there is a Way granting those things.

In practical terms, the ideal politics is the politics of nonaction, where the people believe that the country's prosperity is simply the result of everyone doing well—the kind of good governance where we are not aware that there is someone governing us. When we fall ill with disease, the better treatment is not to take medicine to cure ourselves but to be treated by our own internal vitality. Similarly, capable politics is the kind where problems are resolved through voluntary engagement and active efforts by the public, where we are purified through our self-purification capabilities, where each encourages the other and we prosper without even being aware of it.

After that, there is the politics of action, the politics where we are praised by the people for our good governance, the politics of leaders who are loved and respected. This cannot be said to represent the most excellent and righteous politics.

The most crucial requirement in politics is the trust that exists between a leader and the people. When that trust is absent, people will neither believe a leader even if he or she leads well, nor follow a leader even if he or she speaks the right words. A leader whom nobody follows must use all sorts of ploys and falsehoods to govern his or her country. Governance by leading the people through propaganda and disguise is trying for all, and such a country is destined for misfortune.

Leaders must not lead with words. They must practice in silence, believing in themselves and moving their neighbors with their faith, so that their conviction becomes the key factor in their governance of the nation and its people.

Lecture 18

When Governance through Nonaction Fails

Where the great morals of nonaction collapse,
We set standards with benevolence and righteousness.

When we reveal our wisdom and knowing
The great falsehood rears its head.

When a household is not harmonious
It emphasizes piety and love.

The state in disarray
Emphasizes loyalty.

This section describes four methods of governing a nation and a people.

When politics of morality are well established, goodness and benefits travel continuously throughout society without the need to draw attention to our benevolence and justice. When morals collapse, however, the result is inevitably chaotic and rowdy, as leaders establish and emphasize standards for goodness and assign rewards and punishments accordingly.

Laws may be described as the product of wisdom, but when they are perfectly established, there are bound to be confident men, people who make clever use of them to satisfy private interests and greed. Politics must be politics of morality, of trust in one another.

When one shows only simplicity, the public will be pure and shun artifice. Craft a noose, and there will only be misfortune when the occasion arises to use it.

The happy family's home is filled with love for each other and devotion from children to their parents. When a household is afflicted by problems, the parents are forced to emphasize filial devotion and love. The healthy person needs no prescription, and so he or she needs no medicine. There is a saying: "Let sleeping dogs lie." We often see problems left alone, only for them to escalate greatly because of overreaction when they would otherwise have quieted down by themselves. While artificial efforts to do well are important, a truly crucial method of government is the magnanimity to leave matters to nature. The righteous path in politics is the governance of nature itself, which does not scrutinize or tamper to excess.

The Simplicity of Nature Itself

Forsake the desire to become a wise ruler.
Forsake clever wisdom.
The benefits to the people will be far greater.

Forsake the affectation to be benevolent.
Forsake the bravado to be righteous and just.
The people will return to filial devotion and love.

Put an end to clever feats.
The bands of thieves will dwindle in number.

In these three forms of governance
It is not enough to teach through words and speech.

To make the people follow,
One understands and preserves the ground of truth,
Reduces the personal,
Forsakes ambition.

The benefits to the public are much greater and more numerous than we expect when we let go of sacredness and cast aside the desire to be a good and wise ruler, when we abandon our strategies to become wise. In other words, if we let go of the mind that says, "I must be a good and wise ruler" or "I must produce wise and clever policies," we will not lose our simplicity and the people will actually suffer less.

It is only a hindrance when our benevolence is something we strain to affect, when our rightness is something affected with effort. The mind of the ordinary person carries within it the wish to be devoted to one's parents and loving to one's offspring. The things that are inherently present do not manifest often when we focus solely on formal expressions of benevolence and righteousness. When we leave nature intact, people will return to this devotion to parents and love for children.

In short, my advice is to stop attempting clever tricks and let go of the mind that seeks to benefit. The thief will disappear.

When political leaders seize benefits and seek to be clever, the people will resolve to do the same as well.

These three things cannot be sufficiently taught with words through the scriptures or in schools or through political skill. We must teach them with the power of influence from religious practice and the mind-set based on morals. So when a political leader wishes to have others do as he or she says, that leader must first look within at his or her own mind-ground and show it just as it is, while working outwardly to reduce thoughts and entertain few vain desires.

The Truth Is a Mother That
Feeds All Things

Let go of acquiring knowledge.
There will be no anxiety, no worries.

Is there a lot of difference
Between answers of "Yes, sir" and "Yes"?
How much is the difference
Between the beautiful and unsightly?

This person's fear
Is ever feared by that person.

How humans wander!
Because they have no center in their minds.

How humans rejoice!
Like a great banquet...
Like arriving at a pavilion on a spring day.

I alone have the blandness of no-mind!
With no expression yet on my face,
I am like a newborn baby
Riding forth on the truth!
There will be no other fixations.

People all seem to have their leisure,
Yet I alone seem to search for what is lost;
My mind, like a foolish person,
Seems to not know how to discriminate.

People of the world are clever,
Yet I alone am unclear, unknowing.
People of the world are smart,
Yet I alone seem obtuse.

The broadness, utter broadness!
It seems as wide as the ocean
The exertion without cease!

Like a person who does not know how to rest.

Every person has his or her use,
Yet I alone am stubborn
And thus seemingly without function.

If there is a difference between me and other people
It is that I regard as precious
The truth that feeds all things.

Knowledge is truly a great thing. But when we are bound by it, it becomes a disease. How greatly we are tormented by the presence of cultural diseases in this world! Advancements in knowledge have brought a veritable explosion in cultural disease, yet these diseases emerge and our worries grow, not because knowledge is bad but because we cannot transcend that knowledge or cast aside that fixation. I believe that this anxiety will disappear when we know how to acquire knowledge without fixating and how to use it well where it is to be used.

If you think about it, there really is a great difference between the answers "Yeah" and "Yes, Sir." Yet there are times when it is more suitable between very close friends to simply say "Yeah." It is not the form that matters, then, but the minds of those involved. There is nothing more hollow, however, than politeness without the mind of respect. With wholesomeness and unwholesomeness as well, we may see the two alternating according to perspective and usefulness from one moment to the next. It is their essence that we must understand. We must contemplate to understand the profound origin where no difference exists between wholesomeness and unwholesomeness in terms of their essence.

People decide their fears and their dislikes less by searching within themselves than from the thoughts and fashions of others. How foolish this is!

Why is it that practitioners of the Way and sages sometimes appear thoughtless, indifferent, or foolish, or even chaotic and slightly loopy? It is because theirs is a life of preserving the truth, of constantly yearning for the truth of nonacting nature and attempting to be one with that truth. Worldly people are clever when it comes to identifying their immediate interests, losses, and gains, but the sage pays no mind to these things. Instead, he or she is filled with the mind that seeks the original truth. One has to wonder just how much people truly regard as precious the nonacting truth that is a mother feeding and nurturing all things in the world.

In particular, this section includes a portrait of the sage when he or she is fully engaged in cultivation. The sage does take part in society and engage in efforts as his or her situation demands. At such times, we can find much dignity and discipline, much drive and wisdom. At other times, however, the conditions are not right and the sage rests and exerts in practice. At these times when the sage is exerting in practice alone, he or she may appear somewhat unsophisticated because he or she has transcended external assessments and external matters of interest or right and wrong and is solely focused on practice with adopting the nameless Way suitably as part of him- or herself, yearning for and unified with the Way that is described as a "mother." We must understand that this is not the entirety of the sage's being.

How Did I Find the Truth?

The unlimited face of great grace!
It is simply to follow the principle of great truth.

This one thing called the truth
Seems to exist yet does not, seems to not exist yet does.

Rapture of the truth!
It has a form inside;
Rapture of the truth!
All things live within it.

Tranquil and profound truth!
It possesses precision within.
Precise and true!
Truth manifests belief.
From long ago until today
The names of the sages have not been erased
Because they know the origin of all things.
How might I have understood the origin of all things?
The truth is this mind, now.

There are myriad virtues that arise as the great truth operates. The four seasons cycle through, and as they do, all manner of living creatures live lives of depending on nature. The grace that humans experience from others is relative and conditional, and so we sense that grace. The great virtue that we receive from the truth, however, is absolute and always with us. This is the great virtue without a trace of the virtuous.

Where does it come from, this great and unfathomable grace? It emerges from the Way that is without action. This nonacting truth is described by "this one thing." Yet that object (the nameless Way) is too rapturous to be described as any one thing. It is very confusing. Yet amid that confusion, all things emerge and change through two things: energy that retreats (yin energy) and energy that spreads (yang energy).

The nameless Way is empty. Yet it is not empty within in the same way that an empty space is; it is filled with true energy that cannot be described in words. It is filled completely and minutely, and because of its truthfulness, the changes that occur are necessarily regular and follow with the principles. As a result, we have the sequence of spring followed by summer, fall, and winter, cycling without fail and giving faith to living creatures like the truth.

The teachings of people who became sages through good cultivation of the Way have been passed down to the human societies of today from the distant past. Why do we praise and seek to emulate their virtue? It is because they understand the origin of all things and know how to preserve and make use of it.

What is that truth?

"[It] is this mind, now." We must understand the meaning of this brief phrase. We may say "this" is the news of the truth that cannot be named.

That Which Is Bent Is Actually Whole

That which is bent is actually whole.
When it is bent, it actually stands straight.
When it is hollow, it suddenly surges.
When it is old, it is once again new.
When it is coarsely done, it is actually attained.
When it is many, it is delusive.

Thus the sages,
By preserving the absolute one,
Become standards for the world.

Sages

Strive to not reveal themselves

And thus their names are revealed;

They do not say they are right

And thus their names shine.

They do not boast of what they do

And so their deeds shine brighter;

They are not arrogant

And so they can be the heads.

Sages

Do not compete or contest with anyone.

So in this world

There is no one to compete with them.

It was once said that

That which is bent gains wholeness.

Can these be empty words?

Make the spirit sincerely

And you will return to the truth.

The first section spoke of the "nameless Way" and the "ways that are named." If the nameless Way refers to the essential nature of the truth that cannot be expressed in words, then the principles that bear names speak to the functioning of the nameless truth.

What sort of functioning is that? It is the principle of the two types of energy, of yin and yang.

The universe contains very simple principles that govern all things. These are the two types of action: retreating and spreading. In the spring and summer, it is the principle of spreading that is chiefly at work, and in the fall and winter it is the retreating principle that is mainly operating. This is called the principle of alternating predominance of yin and yang. It is a reference to the interchanging between two types of energy: energy that seeks tranquility and energy that seeks motion.

The ways that are named are a continuation of this motion, of things retreating and then spreading, spreading and then retreating.

This principle applies to all objects in the universe. The minds of humans are also governed by this principle. Sages understand this principle, following what should be followed and managing well what should be used. Ordinary people do not understand this principle, however, and are thoroughly governed in their lives.

The person who works hard in secrecy to prepare will surely be selected by someone and shine; the person who appears to be performing publicly will find his or her problems revealed before long, or will be cut down by others and thereby stopped.

Similarly, modern human culture and civilization originated in Britain and Europe, moving from there to the Americas; now that region is in decline, and the fortunes are shifting toward East Asia. Before long, it may go to India or Central Asia. Similarly, the place of this development will continue shifting. What we must be wary of is the fact that we must abandon the fantasy of our current success or development—or youth—continuing forever. Whether we are declining or returning, we must think deeply before acting. Those who face trials right now must prepare and wait, understanding that if they are constantly readying themselves and amassing virtue now, their time will surely come.

Sages live with the absolute oneness of the nameless truth in their hearts. They regard the principle of alternating predominance of yin and yang as their own standard for living and work in various ways to ensure that they do not decline.

When we are too visible, we commit the misfortune of being forced back, and so we should abstain as much as possible from positions that are elevated and stand out. Even if we are elected by the public and it is inevitable that we are brought into the light, we must have it in mind to immediately step down. In that way, our name will last long and we will have eternal respect.

Sages do not seek to compete with anyone. When a rival emerges, they seek to yield their place. They will yield so that the rival can work, and when the rival steps down, they inevitably appear and work themselves.

Ordinary people always have the comparing mind and objects of competition. The sage does not have that feeling of being in competition or that comparing mind. Thus, there is no one who is his or her equal and he or she wins without a fight.

This message is very much a warning to us. Only by being

humble, by hiding our light and endlessly cultivating the capabilities of nature, can we fatten ourselves for eternity.

The Word That Carries the Way Is Natural

The word that carries the Way is ever natural:
The rough wind cannot blow all morning;
The thundershower does not last all day.

Who is it that does so?
It is the truth.
What the universe does
Cannot last long
With defying the principles;
How much less so a person!

The person who serves the truth well
Is with the person when he or she meets a person of the Way,
Is with them when he or she meets the virtuous,
Is with the person when he or she meets the one who has failed.

The person is with and gladdens the seeker of the Way;
Is with and gladdens the virtuous;
Is with and gladdens him or her who has lost.

Should our faith in being with them be lacking,
There should always be a divide.

Words in accordance with dharma, words without affectation, genuine words—these are always natural. All actions have value when they are of simplicity itself and are without artifice. Forces such as fierce winds and rain inevitably stop before long. In the workings of heaven and earth, that which is unnatural does not last long. This is all the more true for human affairs.

We often speak of how habits tend to last only three days. There are occasions when those who seek to edify and teach others, or to serve others by becoming a political leader, suddenly and unnaturally try to do something well, failing to understand others' position and thinking only of their position so that their attempts to help merely insult others. Or they may seek to do something by force when its time has not come. None of this can ever be true virtue, or the bestowing of genuine grace.

The first thing we must do is to conform to the positions of others. Water adjusts its shape to fit its vessel. It becomes round in a round vessel, square in a square vessel, and runs downhill when the terrain slopes down. True virtue consists of letting go of ourselves and becoming one with the other.

Next, we should try to make others happy. We should help them succeed as befits their situation. Rather than focusing on our own success, we should help the others enjoy the pleasure of succeeding. Happiness comes when we have set our own independent goal, made various efforts to achieve it, and finally attained it. Those who assume responsibility for education or religious work should have the imperative to know how to play the role of midwife, to encourage and assist others as they reclaim morality.

One Cannot Stand Long with Lifted Heels

Lifting our heel,
We cannot stand long.
Walking in broad strides,
One cannot travel far.

Should we seek to reveal ourselves,
We become all the more foolish.
Should we claim that only we are right,
We cannot shine.
The person caught up in boasting of him- or herself

Realizes no real feats.
The person who is arrogant
Is unlikely to be the head.

In terms of morals, this
Is like leftover meal,
Like an unnecessary lump.
So it is that people despise it
And practitioners of the Way do not do so.

We often see banners on the street about how this is "Such-and-Such Week." That focus is observed for a short while, but soon returns to its typical place. Leaps forward quickly crumble when they lack foundation. When we help others, or when we engage in our own affairs, we typically try to do the right thing with a temporary spirit, but it all collapses before long.

We must commit all of our mind and all of our energy to instilling good habits. Once a habit is acquired, it becomes the way we live our daily life. We should not do well simply because we are told to or because we are concerned about someone else's image of us. Instead, we must strive ceaselessly and diligently so that it simply goes well, so that it is simply so. Until a good habit becomes part of our daily life, we must be constantly careful, and we must absolutely refrain from greed or bravado. Ordinary people boast of what they have done, boast of their wisdom, insist only on their own beliefs. They are also resentful when their good deeds go unrecognized, as though they have done something great. Such people are not true practitioners of the Way, nor can they be the virtuous ones who truly serve others.

We must practice righteousness and practice it more, until it establishes itself as a habit and we create righteousness even in our dreams. We must grant virtue to those around us and grant it more, so that it builds up into an immortal tower of merits that no one can tear down. When we boast of this, or when we yearn for recognition, we will soon draw the hatred of others. That is the human mind. The highest standard for practice is to become the master of merit that produces no signs.

The Truth That Contains All Things

There is a truth that contains all things,
That already existed
Before heaven and earth opened.

O tranquil, tranquil truth!
Profound, profound truth!
Standing tall, alone,
It will be changeless forever.

Though this truth works in all things,

It never tires.

It is the mother of heaven and earth and all things.

What name should we give this truth?

Should we name it "the Way"?

If forced to describe it, I would say "it is great."

Great things extend influence in all directions;

The more they do, the farther they grow.

Once they reach an extreme of farness

They return once again.

Viewed in terms of greatness,

The truth, too, is great;

The heavens, too, are great;

The earth, too, is great;

A king, too, is great.

In this broad universe, there are four great things:

The greatness of the king's influence is one of those things.

People model themselves on the mountains and rivers;

The earth follows itself on the energy of heaven;

Heaven follows itself on the truth;

The truth is nature itself.

The one thing of the truth that includes all things existed before the oldest things appeared, heaven and earth. Here, he sings of the Way that was not only there before history began but existed before heaven and earth appeared, the Way that stirs even now for us today, the Way that will exist forever in the eternal future.

All things in the world and the minds of humans in society will change in a myriad of ways, but the truth that transcends time and space is eternal and immortal.

The nonacting Way is eternal, yet by what name should we call it? "Let us call it 'the Way,'" said Laozi, who named it the truth. If we parse the Chinese character for "Way"(道), it is as though the topmost leader has boarded a boat. All things follow the leader in their actions. It has the sense of the "head" of all things, and the path that it follows is principle. Early on, Buddha gave the truth the name of "Dharmakāya," or "law body." He named it so because it was not a physical body but a body of the dharma, a body of truth. Confucius called it "heaven." Heaven, I feel, was meant to indicate some great thing. Founding Master Sotaesan of *Won*-Buddhism gave the truth the name of "Il-Won." This, I think, means that the truth is one, and it contains all things perfectly. What name shall each of us give to the truth?

All of these names are merely the words that we assign and call things by. The truth itself is something so noble and honored that it cannot be defined by a name; it is eternal and exists equally in everything.

The truth is the greatest thing. It is not great in comparison with the small, but absolutely great, embracing all things. It exerts absolute influence on all things, and it follows a cyclical, inexhaustible attitude in which its movements come and go, go and come.

People live their lives emulating and being influenced by their geographical environments, the mountains and the rivers. This is especially resonant as he speaks of the sequence by which the truth is manifested: "The earth obediently follows the energy of heaven, the energy of heaven follows principle, and the nameless Way fills all of nature."

People naturally emulate the mountains and rivers as they create their cultures. If the landscape of a region is gentle, the people who live there will naturally develop a slow and gentle rhythm. When the landscape is strong and sharp, the people will develop a sharp character and a fast rhythm. This happens not because people are doing so deliberately and artificially; they do so without knowing why.

As such, the practitioner must be cautious when choosing a natural environment. We must deliberately decide what to emulate as we go about cultivating ourselves.

Behave with Weight and Tranquility

Weight
Is the root of the light;
Tranquility
Is the head of giddiness.

And so,
Should the sage work all day,
He or she comports himself with gravity.
Should something pleasant happen,
He or she is transcendent amid the festive mood.

All the more
Should the person who governs a nation
Comport him- or herself lightly in the world.
Be light, and he or she loses the people;
Be giddy, and he or she relinquishes power.

Looking at natural phenomena, we see heavy things and light things. Heavy things form the center, while lighter things are subordinate to them. There are also things that are tranquil and things that are excited. Tranquility always functions to make human lives wise and to keep us from losing ourselves. This is something that all of us understand very well. It is difficult, however, to practice this in real life. What good is it to understand? We must have made repeated efforts to practice for tranquility to hold meaning. Sages and great leaders always behave with gravity. If we speak and behave lightly, we frequently come to say different things, causing confusion to those who are led, creating problems in our beliefs and revealing the lack of philosophy behind our actions.

We must be heedful to maintain a transcendent stance and not get caught in the moment. Transcendence becomes rooted in us when we work daily to train ourselves with a tranquil mind, when we adopt a weighty attitude in our discipline and when we place value on the distant future and our own convictions and philosophy. A leader must share in the climate of his or her times and endure the same joy and suffering as the engaged public. If he or she simply plays along with the public without a thought, however, the people will see him or her as someone on whom they cannot depend. We must instill a state of mind that exists alongside them yet transcends them.

Only when we have tranquility and weight and exist in a state transcending reality can we acquire placidity, acquire the grand vision to control reality, and observe phenomena objectively from outside those phenomena as we chart a course to lead.

The Person Who Works
Truly Well

The person who works well
Does well without seeming to do so.
The person who truly speaks well
Does well without finding fault.

The person who counts well
Does not use the abacus.
When the person locks the gate well,
The door cannot be opened, though no bolt has been used.
When a person binds well,

The thing cannot be freed, though no rope has been used.

The sage always does well
To rescue people,
Abandoning no one
And bringing all things to completion,
Abandoning nothing,
And so we call this
The "wisdom of the sage."

The kind person
Becomes teacher to the wrong.
The errant person
Becomes an asset to the kind.

When we do not see teachers as precious,
When we do not love our assets,
Though there may be small wisdom,
The wisdom cannot be called great.
Understanding this and fixing it
Is a marvelous method for completing wisdom.

People live their lives amid work. They succeed when they handle their work well, and they receive payment accordingly. When we are cultivating the Way and studying the truth to become a sage, the message is ultimately that we should do our work well.

Each affair is connected with others and connected to the affairs of the past and affairs of the future. To do our work well, we must not allow these affairs to have a negative influence on other affairs. We must not be in conflict with the past, nor should we have a negative influence on the future. Our affairs must also be beneficial to ourselves, beneficial to others, beneficial now, and beneficial in the future. Doing our work well is truly difficult.

Work here is described as words and calculation and the locking of gates and binding things well. There are other elements here besides work, of course, but if we consider it closely we will see that all things belong to the category of human affairs. We cannot regard some work as fully successful if it is done artificially or unnaturally. Laozi tells us that work should generally be approached through nonaction—that is, its handling should be founded in the Way. We often talk about good and poor handling of work when we speak of orderly justice in society. That matter, however, is to be judged in the distant future once that time has passed. What is right and what is wrong will be judged after all the interested parties have left the scene, based on the spirit of the times (its historical understanding) in light of the situation of the times and from a standpoint that transcends interests. At such moments, we must consider morality. We must consider truthfulness. We must know how to handle our business without sacrificing either morality or truthfulness.

Sages are masters at helping people escape their basic suffering and rescuing them. They will never abandon all people and things. They do not drive people out of their minds or away from their hearts. We cast aside wicked people and we despise the ugly, yet the people who need the guidance of a leader are the wicked and the foolish. Intelligent people and virtuous people have the strength to survive without anyone's rescue. The ones who truly need rescue are the wicked, and so it is that sages extend the deepest attention to each and every one, including these wicked people, striving to make the most of their strengths and help them succeed, and ultimately achieving this. They do not forsake any situation or thing; the sage is a person with the wisdom to commit him- or herself wholeheartedly to attending to wicked people properly and training them effectively.

In structural terms, this world has people in the upper stratum and people in the lower stratum. This is all relative. There would be no upper stratum if there were no upper- and lower-class people. This is why we are supposed to help one another; it is the leader's job to ensure that this happens. The student learns from the teacher, and the teacher practices even more so that he or she can teach the student. If there were no student, the teacher's wisdom and capability would diminish by half. When we fail to understand this and regard our teacher without respect as a student, or fail to love our students as a teacher, we fail to see the broader social structure and the way in which high and low, left and right all assist one another. In terms of time, people may understand now, but in the distant future they will not. We cannot achieve great wisdom with the kind of wisdom that focuses only on formulaic knowledge while failing to understand the principles of change.

Because a great leader embraces all and abandons none, striving unceasingly to learn from them, he or she proceeds to achieve great wisdom.

Guard with the Feminine

Though one is masculine,
Guard it with the feminine
And the hearts of the world shall return.

Oh, valley, where people's hearts gather!
The virtue never leaves it,
Like the newborn without discrimination.

Though one may know clearly,
Guard it with unawareness

And it shall be a model for the world.
Oh, model for the world!
It never defies what is virtuous
And so it returns to the truth without edges.

Though one may be glorious,
Guard it with shame
And it will be a valley where all things gather.
Oh, valley that brings things together!
It is the consummation of loving-kindness,
The original plainness.

Like splitting and shaving the tree into a vessel,
When the sage uses the truth
He or she can be the highest in his or her post.

And, so,
Great governance lies in the mass of truth
That is still undivided.

Even when one possesses masculine stoutness, commitment, courage, pioneering spirit, and drive, the human minds of the world
would naturally return to him or her if he or she preserves it well
with feminine shyness, humility, and softness.

A leader must be both respected and loved. Where there is only respect, there is fear, and people will try to escape from him or her, but they will flock to where there is softness and love. A mother's love must be there for masculinity to gather. If there is simplicity as well, people will gather all the more.

How are softness and simplicity instilled? Internally, we must have a warm heart and take pity on our neighbors. We must also have our eyes open to the truth and understand how to view our neighbors and objects as the conception of a single truth.

Where water is too bright and too clear, the fish will flee. But when someone is truly foolish, people cannot depend on him or her. Fundamentally, we must be bright. We must engage in constant contemplation to become wise. Rather than boasting of that wisdom or impeding the wisdom of others, we should encourage them to think voluntarily, teaching only when there is no other choice. This is a truly difficult thing to do, but it is absolutely required if we are to regard our students as teachers, if we are to hone our students' wisdom and lead others to join together.

Sages see the body of the great truth as they respond to the real world. In their response, they create things that are moral; they create social justice. Throughout this process, the world moves closer to wisdom and virtue. At the same time, one may also become the greatest of elders. All of the different institutions and artificial forms of morality emerged from the original mind that is empty and tranquil. It is in this sense that the expression "splitting and shaving the tree" is used. From this rough material is honed the grand vision and wits and laws to govern society. Great politics, however, must be based in the great nameless Way that never splinters. This is an important principle that leaders must observe: the leader's imperative is such that while he or she may be unwrought material, he or she also knows how to return to the original simplicity.

The World Is a Mysterious Vessel

The ambition that drives us to seize the nation!

It cannot be done through ambition.

The world is a mysterious vessel,

And one cannot make it one's own by force.

Try by force and you will fail;

Keep seeking to seize it and you will lose it.

Objects, in general,

Proceed and follow behind,

Breathe in lightly and breathe out with urgency.

They may be strong and they may be weak;
Some are swept in, some are whittled away.

And so the sage
Acts never in excess,
Lives never in luxury,
Is never great, never arrogant.

There are things in the world that lead one to suspect that a master has been chosen to take responsibility for one's era.

When a master has been decided on for a certain time, people will be unaware, and false people will come forward and seize the moment. Harm will follow and affairs will not succeed. As times change, however, so do masters. When we cling without being aware of this, we will be punished.

The world is not the sort of thing that a political tactician can simply control as he or she feels. The world is alive, and human minds are the truth.

The truth exists with us in the world, and conscience and justice have their eyes open.

Laozi says that the truth breathes within the world. In a sense, it has been decided who will lead and who will follow, who is strong and who becomes weak, whose influence is insignificant and whose is powerful. Things do not succeed when we force ourselves to take on a responsibility that is not our own.

If we aim to rescue the world, we must first practice the truth for the world's sake, making the utmost effort to amass great virtue. We must first act to serve the world.

We must also cast aside selfishness and ambition and return to the pure spirit. To such a person, the time and the opportunity will certainly come.

When sages face the world, they always observe it carefully, diagnosing its condition and preparing a prescription to rescue the world, which they use as a basis as they begin working to salvage it.

Yet while they are turning that prescription into a reality, they do so carefully, revising it as though treating a vessel, as though cooking a young fish in a pot.

Strong Things Wither Swiftly

The person who aids the ruler by the right Way
Will never try to strengthen the country
Through military force,
For the one who enjoys war
Must continue to wage war.

The places where the military rests
Become profuse with brambles.
After a great war
A lean year follows, perforce.

The person who is able at politics
Only produces results through nature;
He or she does not seek to do so through force.
Never boasting of achievements,
Never bragging,
Never arrogant,
He or she is humble,
Treating achievements as accidents,
Never betraying his or her strength.

All affairs and things that flourish will decline.
It is not the proper principles to only act through the strong;
It withers perforce, and swiftly.

When governing a country or managing an organization or household affairs, we may achieve results for the short term by pushing our plans forward by force, but there will immediately come situations in which we cannot handle our affairs with such methods. When we use violence, things become such that they cannot be governed without violence, and violence inevitably persists. We may find such cases in developing countries that face vicious cycles of military coups. This also holds true for education, or for treating disease. We see the same thing when we use a powerful medicine, in that the disease cannot be controlled without more strong medicine. It requires time and a great deal of patience to handle all things according to the principles and ensure their success. But the true leader is one who prepares adequately, helps all people to understand things as possible, and thereby sees to it that we succeed together.

The message is that we should not become arrogant and believe that the leadership of our country or great successes and achievements are purely the result of our own capabilities. Even when we do realize great things, we should recognize the contribution of the public and the care of nature and be humble, very humble. It is human psychology to hate such arrogance and boasting, and it is the providence of the natural order to seek to pull down that which has been ascended. We must have the wisdom and great virtue to share merits and share happiness if we are to become someone strong who endures for eternity without collapsing.

In terms of the seasons, spring and summer are times of flourishing, while fall and winter are seasons of decay. In human affairs and all things, there are times of flourishing, after which come times of decay. Yet the times of flourishing differ in how long or short they are. When flourishing is brief, it is because one seeks to justify the means with the ends or lacks effort and patience. When flourishing is long, it is because one handles affairs according to the right path, makes many efforts, and has much patience. Problems arise when we decide to rush to achieve something because, in so doing, we fall into nature's snare. We must work slowly over time so that we shine one day.

A Weapon Is Never Auspicious

Generally, no matter how magnificent a weapon might be,
It is not auspicious.
It is hated by people, and so
No person with the Way will like it.

The ruler typically
Regards the left as precious,
Yet on the battlefield he or she esteems the right.
A weapon is never auspicious
And so a ruler will not use it.

Should we be compelled to use the military,

We do so transcendently and with a calm state of mind.

Should we win,

We do not regard it as a joy.

To see it as proud is to rejoice in killing.

In general, the person who enjoys killing

Cannot obtain the hearts and minds of the world.

Exalting the left in auspicious affairs,

Exalting the right in inauspicious affairs,

The lieutenant general stands on the left,

The major general on the right.

In war, funerals prevail;

All the people mourn death.

Though we win in war, we should treat it as a funeral.

Laozi was a great lover of peace. Weapons are something feared and hated by all living creatures. They threaten lives, kill, and coarsen the hearts of humans. Living creatures, be they citizens of our country or another, people or microbes, are all precious and have the right to live together in heaven and earth. No one has the right to end life; we may not do with even our own lives—that is a product of the truth.

Weapons of war, which threaten noble lives and are capable of cutting them short, should be done away with forever. Yet the great wealth of countries is used not for loving life and promoting welfare but to develop weapons of war. We should consider deeply how mistaken this is, and I feel it is our duty as human beings to make whatever efforts we can to build a world of perfect peace where weapons need not exist at all.

Even when a war leads to victory, how can that be something for which we can be congratulated or be boastful? No cause or reward can take the place of life. Who can compensate and comfort the parents' pain at their loss, the wife's suffering, the children's grief?

Only the person who repents more after winning, and who has first and foremost the mind of wishing for their future, can be called a great human.

It is said that conducting war should be like conducting a funeral. These truly are cutting words for us.

The Truth Cannot Be Treated as a Subject

The truth can never be named.

Though the workings of the Way are subtle,

No one in this world may regard it as a subject.

Should a king possess the truth,

All things will cheerfully obey of their own accord.

As when the energy of heaven and earth are joined,

The sweet dew falls,

The people are governed on their own

Without any commands.

Should a step be taken forward from the substance and nature of
  the truth
Laws are created, then names of things will be made.
When names are made, standards of values arise.
Stop before you cross the limit.
Know how to stop and you will not be endangered.

The exercise of the Way
Is nature itself,
Like the river flowing to the sea.

The truth cannot be named as any one thing. A name is a conceptual product of ideation in human thought. No noun that has been conceptualized through the human ability to discern and reason can ever be suitable to capture the general nature of the truth. The Way, and the *Il-Won-Sang* truth, is an absolute entity that cannot be named—that is, it cannot be inferred through thought. None of these words, be it the names "Way" or "truth" or "God," is a perfect name, but merely a noun that we use out of necessity.

The functioning of the truth cannot be known because it functions in hiding, yet it is absolutely impossible to defy. We can make that truth part of ourselves, recreate it in our lives, and thereby comply with and use the truth's functioning.

When a political leader has made the truth part of him- or herself and unified with the Way, the public will obey and follow him or her as a matter of course, for he or she will have the might of the truth and possess virtue and wisdom.

There is a heaven and an earth, and people (living creatures) between them. When humans live in peace, their influence extends to heaven and earth so that order is well established in heaven and earth and nature, with good governance and rich harvest years amid suitable sunshine and climate conditions and rainfall. But when people wage war, resentment builds up within living creatures, and when that fury explodes, its influence also extends to heaven and earth in such a way that weather patterns become irregular.

It is said that "laws are created, then names of things will be made." That means that when the nameless and unnameable Way is the origin, we will create all sorts of systems that start from that origin. It is when the state enacts a cultural system in areas such as national law and "mannerly music" that it will finally have a name. One is therefore governing and running a country through laws and manners that bear no artificial names. It is a warning for us not to become too formalized, too fixed, or to forget our original intent and live too much in service of artificial law. When there is too much artificial law, we must have the flexibility to stop immediately and look for a new direction. Otherwise, we could be in peril. I interpret this as a message on the dangers of too rigid a focus on legalism.

If We Do Not Lose Sight of Our Place

When one knows others, we call it wise;

When one knows oneself, we call that sageness.

He or she who defeats others

Is said to have power,

Yet the person who defeats him- or herself is said to be stronger still.

When contented with our place, we are said to be wealthy.

He or she who strives to practice is called a learned gentleman.

If we do not lose sight of our place, we go far.

Even after we die, our merits are not forgotten by posterity;

Our name lives on forever.

All human lives and all human values (such as peace for society) originate first in ourselves. It is when we know others for certain that we know ourselves for certain, and it is when we know ourselves for certain that we can know others for certain. We cannot know others for certain without knowing ourselves. Only the person who knows him- or herself can know others. Thus, the person who claims to know others without knowing him- or herself will have misunderstood the other. More often than not, misunderstandings of others result only in fruitless quarreling.

It is always when we examine ourselves that the light of wisdom shines. We must understand others in that way for us to truly know them well. Thus, it is not wise to know others while remaining uncertain of ourselves; this is not the behavior of a practitioner of the Way. Defeating others is accomplished through power or arms or bravado and other tactics, but there will inevitably be times when we have to lose. We may have defeated others, but if we cannot control ourselves within, we will succumb to failure. In such cases, our defeats of others are rendered meaningless. We also become slaves to ambition when we live our lives through the mind of victory, of seeking to defeat others. The most difficult thing of all is to defeat oneself, and as the power of self-defeat condenses, it moves to other people, nurturing the capability to become our own person.

External riches and power and honor are all very relative, and so we always feel small when compared with someone higher. Moreover, external things are made to relocate constantly over time. We cannot possess them forever, and so our dissatisfaction builds. How can we satisfy this endless human desire? The wealthiest person is said to be the one who knows how to be content with what he or she has now. These truly are wise words.

The Truth Overflows in All Phenomena!

The great truth overflows in all phenomena!
It fills both left and right.
Though it preserves so that all things believe,
It does not speak of its efforts.
Though it brings success by its actions,
It does not remain there.
Though it fosters all things, it does not preside over them.

Being ever without desire,
Can it be called small?

Though it is a refuge for all things,
It does not preside over them
And so it is called great.

And so no sages
Linger after all, even in the greatness,
Thus creating something that is truly great.

The great truth pervades all things. It is with us in every place and
every time. The Way and all things are not separate; all things are
the truth, and the truth is all things. I believe that the person who
is aware of the Way can perceive with his or her senses that the
truth and phenomena are not separate. The Way of nonaction is
also said to operate unfailingly in all things, and to be unlimited in
its grace.

The truth gives all things, yet it does not exist in servitude to
the thought of having given; it creates objects, yet it does not remain in that place alone; it loves all things and helps them grow,
yet it does not interfere with them by force. When humans help
things grow and rescue them and give love, we boast of them instead of being grateful for that grace, and we regard them as our
property. When we consider how many problems this creates in
human relationships, we can see the contrast between the functioning of the artificial and the nonacting truth.

The truth works alone, yet because it declines and transcends the credit for its work, we say that it does not exist. For this reason, there is no word that can accurately capture how great it is. This means that even while the sages who have awakened to this truth and put it into practice are engaged in the great and sacred work of delivering the world, they can actually be called great because they have transcended that greatness and sacredness.

Water flows downhill. Why should water flow downhill? Because there is a principle by which heavy things travel downward. That principle also exists within water. Even very small matter does not simply sit there; it rots or transforms. That is constant transformation, which occurs because there exists a principle of transformation in all things. A person who is aware of the Way and how it fills all the myriad things will see, while the person whose mind-eye is closed will not. Our mind-eye must be open to see the truth.

Songs and Music Make a Person Stop

When we grasp and practice the great truth
We can go anywhere in the world
And be at ease without encountering any harm there,
Peaceful and carefree.

Songs and music make the passersby stop,
But the place where the truth is practiced
Is so bland that it cannot be said to have any flavor.

Though we see the truth, we cannot be said to have seen it all.

Though we hear it, we cannot be said to have heard it all.

Though we use it, we cannot use it all.

People who possess power will have people obeying and entertaining them wherever they go. That power, however, will not remain long with them. It will seek to go elsewhere, or others will seek to wrest it away. We are forced to work very hard to guard it. We have to be wary of others, and if we exert the power wrongly the devastation is great.

What about the person with money? The power of money has always been great, but keeping it is an agonizing affair, and the money will constantly seek to roll away somewhere else. Stopping that is utterly impossible.

Worldly values with forms, such as power and money, have limits to them. When they transform, they are utterly fleeting, so that when money and power collapse, the person who owned them very often collapses along with them.

There is no one, however, who can take away the truth once a person possesses it. There is no one who will envy it, and the more we give the truth we possess to others, the higher and more esteemed we will be. It is also the kind of mysterious possession that can be used by anyone in any place and at any time. When we possess this truth, we can create a heaven, ultimate bliss, and paradise in our mind. Thus we can always experience pleasure, regardless of the world. The person who possesses the mysterious truth will also be welcomed by others that he or she meets because he or she spreads peace and warmth and wisdom to those around. There may, however, be many people who do not understand it. He or she may also become an object of hatred for people who stubbornly insist on old values alone, but fundamentally he or she will give grace to them.

Sensory pleasure may be good momentarily, but it makes us heedless. It arouses primitive desires, it makes us lazy, and it drags us into a world without value. But those who do not experience pleasure in being awakened to and practicing the truth find it difficult to see such attributes of sensory pleasures. We can liken it to popular songs, which we can enjoy easily and sing along to, and classical music, which is difficult to sing along to. Understanding and experiencing the Way is something that only truly sincere people can do. And because it is truly inexhaustible and unlimited, the person who understands it will experience true pleasure, while its door will remain closed to those who are ignorant or unskilled and those who pursue pleasures.

The Truth Gives First

If the truth wishes to gather from you in the future,
It gives to you first.
If the truth wishes to make you weaker in the future,
It makes you stronger first.

If the truth wishes to bring failure to you in the future,
It makes you thrive first.
If the truth wishes to take away from you in the future,
It gives to you first.
Whoever knows this is said to be wise to the mechanism of the truth.

There is a principle whereby the flexible
Vanquishes the strong.
Like the fish that cannot leave the pond,
All things cannot escape this principle.

Thus we are told
To not show off the conveniences of our country.

The law of the truth is that when things are big, they grow smaller, and when things are smaller, they will grow in the future. When
things move, things rest, and when things have rested, things
move. In this way, things cycle inexhaustibly, but when things
reach the extreme, things return to where they were.

If we observe the workings of heaven and earth and nature, or
of the world, we see that those who give receive and those who
receive give. Weak things become strong again. After becoming
full, the moon gradually wanes to become a crescent, which proceeds back toward a full moon. We must read these changes appropriately. For these phenomena contain within them a principle
known as the "mutual pushing" of yin and yang.

The person who lives his or her life unaware of this sequence
and these laws of change will live a frantic life being taken in by
these changes. The person who understands this principle well,
in contrast, will have a good understanding of its mechanism and
travel safely on his or her road. He or she can also use the mecha-

nism to build peace and comfort for the world.

We experience countless tests as we live our lives. The tests that are given regularly at school present few problems, since we only need to prepare for them. But when we are confronted by society in our lives, we experience tests that are unexpected and unplanned. We are tested by random things with the people who exist above and below us in the social hierarchy.

It is only when we pass these tests safely that we can take on great things. A great leader will be presented with gateways in the form of more tests.

Sometimes people are offered tempting forms of bait that test their honesty and judgment, their ability to break through, or their transcendence. To pass these tests, we must discipline ourselves well with our moral sense on a day-to-day basis, and we must understand the subtle principle of change in all things. Only then can we become a great and eternally powerful leader who is not content with small things.

The Truth Is Simple

The truth never seems to be working

Yet there is nothing in which all things are not governed.

When the ruler emulates the workings of the truth,

All things will transform of their own accord.

Should too much desire to edify arise,

I will overcome the artificial with simplicity.

The simplicity of the truth

Possesses no artificial desires.

Seek to overcome desire with tranquility

And that land will rectify itself of its own accord.

The truth seems to not be operating, yet it is sincerely functioning at all times, transforming all things and governing the universe. There is probably no person in existence who can match the truth in its diligence. The truth's movements are such that it works and yet seems to not be working. This is possible because it has no selfish desires.

When a leader is guiding an organization, it is much like the working of the truth: If he or she deliberates with the organization's members to chart a course and operates naturally with a mind that is simple, rather than making a big show of artificial leadership and "accomplishing something," his or her efforts will be successful. To live our lives with this kind of simplicity, we must cultivate our spirits to overcome our selfish desires and attain the tranquility that is the origin of simplicity.

What can a leader do to escape difficulties that arise from the operation of selfish desires as he or she goes about his or her business? This is not a matter that can be resolved through money or power or other tactics. Instead, the prescription recommended here is simply to recover the pure mind of the truth and overcome problems in a moral way. When we face a difficult situation, we will only encounter greater trouble when we lie or use violence to avoid it. It is a situation that demands recovery of truthfulness above all else. What can we use to clean and purify our tainted mind? When we return to nature and bask in the sounds of birds and water, the unaffected scenery, we feel that our minds have become clean. Yet an extremely tainted mind may travel briefly to be with nature, only to have all those effects wiped away. We must therefore engage daily in mind-practice to make our mind tranquil before we can cleanse that which is tainted in our mind.

Great Grace Is Not Virtuous

High virtue does not seem virtuous,
Yet its grace manifests eternally.
Low virtue seems virtuous,
Yet it may cause harm because of this grace.

Ultimate grace is nature itself;
There is nothing to which it is not granted.
Low grace is artificial;
The extent of that grace is limited.

True loving-kindness is unaffected—
A love without any conditions.
Though we may call it great righteousness,
Righteousness possesses the extreme.
With utter decorum, we behave decorously.
Yet when there is no answer
We seek to enforce decorum, even if we must drag people by the arm.

After losing the truth of nonaction, then,
Our standard is inevitably virtue.
Losing virtue,
Our standard is inevitably benevolence.
Losing benevolence,
We follow etiquette and form.

In general, what we call etiquette
Is a dependence on form that arises
When truthfulness and faith are shallow.
It is the greatest at confounding the truth of nonaction.

The intellectuals of old
Loved only the beautiful shell of manners
And so they made the world foolish.
Thus the great man
Preserves the realm of truth closely
Yet is unbound by form,

Practices the truth substantively
Yet does not stroll about in the beauty of words.

And so practitioners
Choose the true and forsake shells.

The person who awakens to the unnameable Way and shapes his or her character with it is said to be a sage who has achieved great virtue. The word "virtue" here is an expression with the same sense of "loving-kindness" or "love." The highest level of this loving-kindness and love is called "high virtue." When viewed from the side that grants love, this high virtue is the mind of the parent's pure love for a child, without any trace of the mind of having granted love and without any notions of demanding conditions or compensation. Also, we always offer the best gifts for a person's situation when giving love. We restore humanity and give loving-kindness with philosophy, loving where love is to be given, and being critical where criticism is demanded. At times, we may be strict, distant, or close. The gift of grace is varied and essential, centered on the person receiving it, often with the recipient being left unaware to avoid any burden. Of course, there may be times when he or she is made aware as necessary for educational purposes.

There are times when a parent is expressing love for his or her child that the parent's values are too deeply manifested, or unwise love is given that ultimately causes the child's future to turn out unfavorably. The sage's loving-kindness, however, is accompanied by wisdom and never creates obstacles to the future of any sentient being. Parents may also give love to their own child while failing to do so for the children of others. The sage, in contrast, always gives the appropriate love to people with whom he or she has affinities, and even those with whom he or she does not.

The truth grants a nonacting loving-kindness to all things. Humans act in ways characterized by artificial values such as "virtue," "benevolence," "righteousness," or "politeness." Artificial virtue is virtue, clearly, but it may be a burden to the recipient, and even the person exhibiting the virtue in question may experience something of a mind-set of compensation, making things go awry because of that virtue. Moreover, this virtue may actually harm real virtue because it is not fundamental and because it is only partial and not eternal.

When politeness veers toward involuntary formalities and affectation without the respect that is the foundation of etiquette, it may become a frame that binds the human being's free mind-nature or result in inhumane situations that impoverish the human being's abundant stores of feeling.

Yet when their true intent is well preserved, it is problematic for us to think lightly of politeness, righteousness, benevolence, and virtue, and superior virtue functions as superior virtue by way of the benevolence, righteousness, and politeness that humans are bound to observe. It is therefore the proper sequence for the person whose character is not yet mature to first practice formal benevolence, righteousness, and politeness, even if it seems burdensome and frustrating, before eventually achieving the high virtue in which he or she has shed any sense of compensation. We must therefore be aware that extreme liberalism or naturalism that defies the proper social order is a far cry from what Laozi truly intended.

The Truth Is One

Since long ago, all people
Have obtained the truth that is one.

Heaven is clear because it attained the one truth;
The earth is peaceful because it attained oneness;
The spirits are numinous because they attained oneness;
The valley may be full because it possesses oneness.
All things arise because of this one truth;
Leaders obtain this one truth;
And so they can be fair.

All of these things
Arose through this one truth.

Being grounded in oneness, the heavens will break apart if not clear.
Being grounded in oneness, the land will be disturbed if not peaceful.
Being grounded in oneness, the spirits will rest if not numinous.
Being grounded in oneness, the valley will run dry if it cannot be
  filled.
Being grounded in oneness, all things will perish if they cannot create.

Being grounded in oneness, the king who is not right
Will not be able to stand nobly.
Oh, emulation of the truth,
The noble places its roots in the base;
The high places its roots in the lowly.
The king calls himself
A lonely person, an inadequate person, a person without blessings.
Such things
Are all seeking to be rooted in the base.

Is it not so;
The ultimate honor is to be without honor.
Wish not to glisten like jade;
Live humbly like the rolling stone.

This section speaks of how all things are grounded in the truth, how even though heaven and earth and living creatures and objects show different characteristics as they form and transform, those characteristics cannot manifest apart from the one truth. What, in particular, are the characteristics of a political leader? He or she must be the ground in which all things are sown, and so his or her characteristic is humility.

Nature proceeds according to characteristics, but in the case of humans the attitude of one's mind becomes an issue for kings, queens, and leaders. Humility is emphasized here because this characteristic of a king or queen may be forgotten.

Ordinary people do not think at all of the truth that fills the universe. The person who practices the Way commits his or her whole heart and energy to finding that one truth. The sage has awakened to this truth and uses it as a standard when acting and teaching others. All people—those who understand, those who do not understand, and even inanimate objects—are rooted in that one truth and live under the truth's command. If we understand and comply with this aspect of the truth, applying its principles from time to time in our lives, the world will be a haven and ultimate bliss. Those who are governed by the truth without being aware of that truth, however, will find themselves living lives of suppression under a tyrant or dictator.

Existing as they do and grounded in the one Way, heaven, earth, living creatures, and all things naturally acquire its characteristics: virtue appears as the sky is clear, the earth is at peace, and spirits are wondrous. The Way that governs all things may be one, but its virtues manifest in distinctive ways according to the characteristics of all things. So when all things cast aside the one truth, the virtue of these things cannot manifest.

The truth that governs heaven and earth takes the high and brings it low, takes the low and makes it high, takes the humble and makes it noble, and takes the noble and makes it humble. This is the Way of nature manifested from the one truth. To understand this principle ahead of time and acquire its nobility for a long time, we must behave in a low and humble way—that is, with humility and diligence—so that our nobility can long be sustained. What we have will also go away, and what we lack will be made replete. When the one who has plenty enjoys giving to others, his or her possessions may be eternal.

Returning When Things Have Gone as Far as They Should

To return when things go as far as they should
Is the motion of the truth.
To transform gradually in subtlety
Is the sequence of the truth's working.

The myriad objects
Arise from the existing.
The existing arose from nonexistence.

The bitter winter cold always changes direction when it reaches an extreme. The same is true for the summer heat: when it reaches an extreme, it changes direction and becomes cold again. So it is with human successes, which stop at the extremes. Conversely, sadness too changes course toward joy when it reaches its extreme. This is the law of the action of the truth. Its process, in which things are made to turn around and reach another extreme, results in constant, very subtle changing. As this builds up, an extreme is reached. Even the long winter nights shorten by very small measures from one day to the next, until the summer solstice comes and the night reaches its shortest. The truth proceeds minutely without resting, and when it reaches as far as it can, the time comes to change directions and return.

This movement—the going and then coming back, coming and then going back—does not happen because anyone commands it to. It is a motion of the Way, which happens on its own accord. It is not done artificially but is the spontaneous working of the truth through nonaction. The intervals of change in this movement of heaven and earth are very precise and can be measured through the four seasons.

Changes in human society also take place according to this principle of return and minute activity. Nature is mechanical, and so its changes are easily predicted through the four seasons and such. Because of the mutability of the mind's actions, however, changes in individual humans do not have precise intervals of return and minute activity, but changes ultimately take place according to the two principles. If a person is too focused on his or her work, for example, a state of return will emerge that tells him or her that it is time to rest. If we rest too long, another mind will tell us that it is time to work again, and we will start working. There may, however, be differences in how this changing direction manifests in people according to their psychological state. The speed of transformation may also be very gradual, with very small steps for some people, but others may progress relatively quickly, depending on their personality.

In terms of social change, too much flourishing will lead to signs of corruption and degeneration within society, which will gradually spread until they ultimately bring about decline.

The myriad objects of the world all emerged from the two energies of yin and yang, and those two energies are said to have emerged from the nameless Way at a time before they had been divided. This can be understood as the reverse of the explanation in the first section, in which the nameless Way is described as originating from heaven and earth and truths with names are said to be the matrix of all things.

That Which Is Very Innocent Appears Cloudy

Advanced scholars hear the truth
And work diligently to put it into practice.
Ordinary people hear the truth
And sometimes practice it and sometimes don't.
Foolish people hear the truth and laugh it off as vain.

The principles that foolish people do not scoff at
Cannot be called the right truth.

And so, among the words passed down from long ago,

Bright truth is said to appear vague,
Advancing truth seems to retreat.
Even truth seems uneven.
Great grace seems absent, like the empty valley.

What is greatly innocent is said to appear cloudy.
Broad virtue seems inadequate.
Fair grace seems feeble.
Simple truth seems fickle.

What is greatly edged is said to have no corners.
The great vessel arises belatedly.
The great sound rarely makes a sound.
The great form has no form.

Truth, being hidden in all things,
Cannot be named.

What is there like the truth
That lends of itself
To create all things?

Sages awaken to the original nature by making their minds tranquil and unifying with the original realm of objects. They also
engage in constant contemplation to understand the myriad prin-

ciples. These are then presented as doctrines, words, and dharma instructions that come from examining the societies of the distant future and human minds and are applied to the lives of people. All sages, then, come to possess their own records of their words and deeds, their own systematic scriptures.

Students at a high level have no difficulty hearing the content of these scriptures and awakening to and practicing them. Intermediate students have a mixture of belief and skepticism, and may practice them or not. People who have no interest at all in the Way laugh at the content and dismiss it as false or impossible.

When those who are ordinary or at an intermediate level observe the words of the sages and the actions of the people who revere them and put them into practice, they may find some things that seem incomprehensible in the minds of ordinary people or those at an intermediate level.

As an example, there are instances where the truly radiant also appears to be very vague. Black-and-white logic is clear, simple, and explicit, but situational logic, in contrast, is somewhat ambiguous, and those who do not possess complex thinking will regard it as vague because their own intellectual ability is low.

To truly succeed, we must have broad discernment. In such cases, however, we examine all things and solidify the fundamentals and the foundation without being stubborn. At first glance, we may even seem to be going backwards.

True equality is not simple straight-line equality but practical equality that is clear from one situation to the next. It is by no means equality to give the same to the person who has gone without food for a day and the person who has merely missed a meal.

The grace of parents is the granting of grace in which we lament not being able to always provide for our children. The loving-kindness of the sage may seem feeble because the sage entreats the public as he or she gives and offers teaching.

Being simple and maintaining constancy allows us to respond to any situation without being bound by formality, since we are confident in ourselves, and to show what may outwardly appear to be great fickleness because we never lose sight of the essence.

The truth is hidden in all things, constantly providing what is necessary to all things. It divides its grace properly for its objects and does not demand repayment. This is why the truth's grace is great and the loving-kindness of the sage is limitless—because he or she has adopted that truth as a model in his or her cultivation.

The Sequence of
the Truth's Transformations

The truth gives birth to oneness.
Oneness gives birth to two.
Two, in turn, gives birth to three.
Three gives birth to all things.

When all things carry yin energy,
Embrace yang energy.
It harmonizes these two energies,
Realizing constant change.

The things people despise
Are lonely, inadequate, and unwholesome.
Kings and lords call themselves
By these names.

And so
What we call the principle of objects
Is added when subtracted,
Is subtracted when added.

What people teach
I, too, teach.

The person who boasts of strength
Cannot die in comfort.
I, too, regard my lowness
As the greatest teaching.

The truth is one. God in Christianity, the Buddha nature in Buddhism, heaven in Confucianism, and *Il-Won* in *Won*-Buddhism all return to the same object, differing only in name. The object of truth explored in the sciences and the object of truth that we seek to awaken to in religion are one. It is only the methods of exploration that differ, and the matter of whether the scope of their use applies to all matter or only humanity.

This truth is one in the origins of the principles that govern the universe. When it functions, however, we may observe it in the form of two energies: contracting yin energy and expanding yang energy. The third energy is one that harmonizes the two. Like the "mainstream," "non-mainstream," and "centrist" that we find in the world, we may speak of three energies, the yin and yang energy and the energy of the middle harmony that harmonizes them. It is through this that creative transformation occurs and all things are produced and grow.

All objects have centripetal and centrifugal forces, such that individual objects preserve and sustain their forms as they live thanks to the harmonious energy that seeks to complement and complete them.

It was previously stated that the incarnation of the Way that acts as the foundation for the universe is a single entity, but that when it operates properly it exists as two entities, and that the proper harmony of the two represents a third. What are we to emulate in our practice as we observe this existential phenomenon? We must draw some ideas from this. The application of the principles in our own lives is referred to as morality and the mind-dharma of the sages; Laozi looked at the single principle and instructed us to train our mind to be empty and calm. This is presented as an exhortation for us to adopt as our model of the Way of yin and yang. Yang takes the form of expansion, while yin takes the form of contraction, yet these two energies change once they reach an extreme. In the same way, our leaders are taught to embrace decline if they wish to happily expand, living always with the contraction and humility that are yin virtues. This is why the king and queen are said to have adopted the form of lowering themselves and describing themselves as "lonely" people or as being "at fault." This shows that Laozi also regards the mind-dharma of humility and self-lowering as the greatest of teachings that all of us in the world may understand.

Softness Governs Hardness

The softest thing in the world
Governs the hardest of things,
For that which is without form
Can penetrate even where there are no cracks.

And so I
Have understood that the greatest benefit in the world
Is that which does through nonaction.

The teaching that is unspoken,

The benefit of doing without action—
Those who have mastered this mind-dharma are rare.

When one is moving people's minds and leading them to do good things, it is not effective to use power or punishment or spears and swords that threaten. What is truly effective is when we do so with gentle love and loving-kindness. Gentleness is akin to life force. Consider the soft sprout of the young plant—how its life force abounds! But the rigid is akin to death. Consider the stump of a dead tree—it is extremely stiff. The frail water defeats the rigidness of rock. We must also understand the feminine softness that controls rigid masculinity.

When we are working hard for ourselves and society, it is truly difficult to avoid boasting, to do it quietly and properly understand the context. It is only possible when we have put a tremendous amount of effort into our mind-practice, and we can only do it when we lack a desire for honor and material things, when we know how to examine the moment and we understand the other party.

As our practice accumulates over a long period of time, things succeed on their own without us making an effort. When we make many preparations, we can do our work placidly with humility and forbearance. With advanced discipline, we reach the point where we act without acting.

In teaching others, the unskilled person teaches with words. It is important to provide a model by practicing what we teach, and it is a more skillful teaching still that takes place through the mind and energy. If we are filled with the state of love and respect for the other, minds connect and are moved without any words

It Is Not Dangerous
If We Know How to Stop

Which should we hold more dearly: honors or the body?
Which should we treat as more precious: the body or money?
Which is more sickening: gaining or losing?

Where attachment is deep, we consume more things.
When we hide many things, we lose greatly.
Know how to find contentment and there will be no disgrace.
Know how to stop and there will be no danger.
Could you but live this way,
You would be at peace forever.

The words offered in this section allow us to live a truly meaningful life even when it is ordinary. The people of the world rush this way and that, roaming about while pursuing honors and interests. So fixated are they on external things that they become playthings of "more" and "less," "high" and "low," yet they continue flailing busily without being aware of this.

When we possess many honors and a great deal of money, we must concern ourselves with preserving them in various ways, and as a result the disease of arrogance arises. Arrogance forces us to lose sight of our true self. The mind that seeks to preserve riches is the culprit responsible for our distance from others. It functions to devastate our spiritual ability and ultimately results in us abandoning ourselves.

If we can rein in and halt the state of mind that is racing with excessive desire, if we can calm our lust for honors and money, then we can be said to be a great person who is true to our life.

The external life is a life of helping others live. The most important thing of all is to tend truly well to ourselves as we live. If we can train a mind that is rich and abundant and manage our body so that it remains healthy, external honors, riches, and power will follow. Due to the fact that the external is nothing more than a series of things that we should exhibit command over and use well, becoming bound by the external results in a life of putting the cart before the horse.

Great Eloquence Seems Inarticulate

That which is greatly complete seems to be flawed
Yet there is no vice in its use.
That which is full seems to be empty
Yet there is no exhaustion when we use it over and over again.

The great and straight seem bent.
The skillful seems petty.
Great eloquence seems inarticulate.
Tranquility vanquishes haste.
Coolness vanquishes passion.

And so
The mind-dharma that is clear and tranquil,
It will set the world right.

What is the character or capability of the sage? He or she possesses an attractive power in which his or her apparent flaws and deficiencies lead those around him or her to try to compensate for them. Yet the smart person, the person who is successful in a worldly manner, possesses no empty spaces. For this reason, he or she is feared, and thus lonely. When those who approach the sage to compensate because the sage seems deficient, the sage embraces them well. Thus, the sage can add more to his or her wisdom, and the sage becomes inexhaustible because he or she can make use of various things.

The sage seems bent, shameful, inarticulate; at times, he or she is quiet and cold. All of these things represent placidity. They regard the wisdom of others as their own wisdom, know how to accept what belongs to others, proceed forward when they appear to retreat, and move in a fitting way that follows how things go.

To be disciplined to attain such a character, they must meet the right teacher and receive his or her instruction well. They must awaken to the truth of the universe, regarding it as their textbook and striving inwardly while working outwardly to hone their capability to judge and adjust objects appropriately. In other words, a great deal of effort is required. Thus, someone such as Confucius said that proper governance occurs when such a person is found and that governance is poor when such a person is not found. Let us become that person. Let us become owners of a character that is absolutely essential.

True Satisfaction

When a country is governed well with the dharma,
Swift horses will feed the soil.
When a country is governed wrongly,
Warhorses will bear young at its borders.

Unhappiness arises from not knowing how to be satisfied;
Faults arise from seeking to possess by force.

And so
It can only be called true knowledge of satisfaction
When we are content to know gratitude for all things.

In a peaceful and well-run country, the strongest horses are used for agriculture. In a poorly run country, however, horses suffer from giving birth on the frontier battlefield because of war. This appears to be the result of excessive desire and the presence of unwise people as leaders.

Our desires ultimately set us aflame and leave the world in disorder. Human desire knows no limits, and when we live by those desires, we are likely to succumb to the mire of suffering. Desire in a leader not only creates hardship for members of his or her organization but also causes misfortune for the public, meaning that they cannot see properly and end up making poor decisions. People also become angry because their desires are not met, leading them to become violent and coarse. As we try to satisfy our desires by force, we act out falsehoods and employ deception. All of our efforts fail because of this desire to commit acts by force that would otherwise be impossible.

The more desire we have, the further we grow from a peaceful state of mind; the stronger our fixation on desire, the more suffering follows. Buddhist monk Wonhyo once said that greed was the reason why so many people went to hell, where there is no temptation, and so few people proceed to ultimate bliss, to which no one blocks the path. If we were to focus our lives on having a peaceful state of mind, living life as it comes without any desires, we might feel at ease, but we would also be left incapable of dealing with the world. We would become someone who does nothing of service for the world, a complacent, easygoing person.

Laozi delivers a serious warning here, as nearly all politicians and leaders have acted out of reverence to excessive desire. When used properly, desire actually results in self-improvement, and noble desires are the driving force leading us to develop great capabilities. What remains important, however, is that we know how to train desire effectively and set the proper course to bring positive values into being. We must have the ability to manage and control this desire properly, and we must strive particularly hard to sublimate that desire well into a great and noble vow. If we are becoming a slave to desire at this moment, we must know how to cut our desire down to size and content ourselves with what we have now, thus achieving a peaceful state of mind.

Knowing the World without Venturing Out

Without venturing outside the house,
We know the things of the world.
Without looking outside the window,
We see into the truth of the universe.

The more we roam outside, the further the truth drifts away.
The more sundry our knowledge, the more fragmented our
  knowledge is.

And so the sage

Can know without necessarily executing.
Can name without necessarily seeing,
Can achieve without effort.

This section explains the wisdom and capabilities of the sage. The sage understands the principles of the universe's operation through the principles within him- or herself. When we master these principles and discipline ourselves with tranquility and trenchant wisdom, we come to understand the rise and fall, prosperity and degeneration of the world.

This ability is not something possessed by sages alone; all humans have within them a lantern of wisdom. The only difference is that ordinary people use it where it is not necessary and are scattered in their senses, whereas the sage uses it where it is necessary for humankind and inherently gathers and applies it.

In the first section, it was said that the sage always awakens to the essential nature of the universe from the stage that is free of thoughts and always understands changes in objects through thinking and contemplative activity. We ought to consider whether we are doing the same.

We should also consider what it is that we are striving to understand. It is important to consider questions such as "What is the object of my contemplation?," "What should I do to create objects well?," and "What do I have to do to make a positive impression on my boss?" The truly relevant thing, however, is striving to awaken our own mind. Once we awaken it, we have all of the principles of the outside in our mind. When we light the lantern of our own mind, we can then reflect its brightness on things and understand everything about them.

When we strive greatly to retain the knowledge shared with us by others, it may add to our storehouse of knowledge but it does not produce the wisdom that generates such knowledge ourselves. When we seek to externally understand what belongs to others, the internal wisdom that flows out from within us becomes forever darkened. The interior naturally becomes darkened because our lantern is only used to illuminate the outside. Thus, it is true that the wisdom of the sage will only diminish the farther we roam in search of it. The lantern of wisdom exists within our own minds. It is an agent of understanding, a specific object that we can describe as an "intellectual actor." When we shine it only on faraway places, the agent of understanding weakens and we become internally foolish. Cultivating a mind that applies force and fuel where the specific object of understanding lies is thus a shortcut to illuminating internal wisdom.

Shadows follow people wherever they go. To eliminate a shadow, we need to become the light source ourselves and it will go away. It is only by focusing attention on becoming a light source in this way that we will obtain the wisdom of the sage.

It is said that those who hone wisdom achieve understanding of fundamental principles. When we have this capability in our wisdom, we acquire the miraculous power to understand the causes of things as though we see them without actually seeing them, to understand merely by hearing, to send influence to different places without venturing there ourselves, and to handle affairs properly through our own power of mind.

To Reach 'No Mind'

Study sciences and your knowledge compounds by the day.
Study the truth, and defilements and idle thoughts dwindle by the
  day.

Reduce and reduce and you will reach the stage of no-mind.
When you achieve nonaction, what is there that you cannot do?
Though you attain and govern the world,
You will govern from the realm of no-mind.

If there is even the slightest

Mind of boasting,
One cannot govern
In contentment with the world.

When we study sciences, our knowledge grows by the day. But when we practice the Way, defilements and idle thoughts disappear.

The way to making people happy and becoming a leader, however, is not through broadening knowledge. To make our mind clean and pure and hone our wisdom, it is far more beneficial to practice the truth.

If academic studies are typically a matter of acquiring phenomenological knowledge in which the objects of study lie outside, then practice with the study of the Way is a matter of unifying with the substance and essential nature, thereby achieving an empty state of no-mind by eliminating all of the miscellaneous ideas and signs, defilements and idle thoughts. And because the object of our practice is within the internal mind of our ego, there arises the capability of nonaction in which we understand the "method of mind management"and can use all knowledge outwardly.

It is indispensable to study sciences outwardly, and it is also indispensable to study the truth (mind-practice) internally. Ultimately, I believe that we must engage in both forms of study. In terms of sequence and focus, however, we should proceed first with studying the Way, where our own internal self-management is central, and then use this as a basis for studying knowledge. While it is very difficult to proceed from the outward study of knowledge toward practice with the truth, one can achieve excellent outward study of knowledge if one engages in mind-practice (studying the Way) internally.

Studying the Way is a better process for bringing one's self in line with the truth. At the ultimate stage, we will achieve free command over our desires and reach an ultimate bliss or paradise without defilements or idle thoughts. It is also a practice aimed toward embodying moral politics, as the free management of our minds allows us to lead without losing the leader's imperative or defying the truth (the Way) in our judgments of things.

In reality, the politicians that we see exist in service of desires as they govern or are dominated by their own sense of honor or a thirst for honor and hearing the praises of others. In the end, we cannot trust the government to people whose actions cater to greed or interests or the "self-sign" and pretensions. We must therefore become sage politicians, leaders who are true people uncontrolled by greed and arrogance, and we ought to find such people to foster them and entrust them with important affairs.

When the Attached Mind Is Absent

The sage has no fixed mind.

What the people want, he or she regards as his or her own mind.

Meeting a kind person,

He or she does so with a kind mind.

Though he or she meets someone wicked, he or she does so with a

kind mind.

This is the great kindness of the sage.

Meeting a trustworthy person,

He or she gives full faith.
Meeting a person who cannot be trusted,
He or she does so with faith.
This is the great faith of the sage.

When a sage exists in the world,
He or she carefully gathers the views of the people
Until finally he or she becomes one merged with the people.
The world focuses its eyes on the sage;
The sage regards the people as children one and all.

In the *Diamond Sūtra*, the Buddha uses the phrase "there is no fixed dharma," meaning that "the truth that is not fixed in anything is the buddhadharma." There is also the teaching that the true buddhadharma means not being bound to the idea of the Buddha's dharma. This is the same as what is referred to as the sage's "no fixed mind." Possessing such a mind, the sage may be recognized and receive the respect of the public, yet he or she does not become intoxicated by this, such that his or her mind becomes excited or clamorous. He or she focuses on guarding the simple inherent mind, responding in a natural way as though nothing ever happened.

Sages are not bound by anything. They are not limited to anything, nor are they trapped in the formulaic. That is because they stroll at a stage of no-thought. Ordinary people exist in service to physical desires, to the desire for honors, to the desire to increase their number of possessions. Because of this, because they are fixated on stagnant ideas that they have established, they remain unfree internally while living a life of resentment outwardly.

Because of their desires and fixations, ordinary people are always focused on the self, self-centered in their judgments and affairs. As such, they do not know to think of the situations of others; even if they do think of others, they help those others in a self-centered way. Thus, it is that true help rarely occurs in the world. Sages, strolling at a stage of nonaction, are capable of seeing the world correctly and becoming true leaders who benefit others and the world as a whole.

Sages live a life of guiding and edifying the world, of placing others at the center.

Sages cast aside their own desires and comfort and honors, regarding the minds of humankind as their own mind and living lives of sacrifice in which they turn the wishes of society into their own wishes.

Because they understand the extremely kind truth is inherent in human nature, sages understand and seek to develop the nature of the people with whom they interact. They can therefore treat un-wholesome people as wholesome, guiding even those who they do not understand with a state of mind of constant faith until such time as that nature is restored.

People Who Die Badly

People are born and proceed toward death.

Three of every ten live well;

Three of every ten die well;

Three of every ten

Are born and act as humans,

Only to meet death having done wrong.

What is the reason when we die having done wrong?

It is excessive fixation on life.

I have heard it said that
He or she who practices well to cultivate life
Ventures forth on the road
Yet meets neither bison nor tigers,
Ventures into the military
Yet bears neither armor nor weapons.

Meeting a rhinoceros,
He or she is not struck by the horn;
Meeting a tiger, he or she is not scratched;
Meeting an enemy soldier, he or she is not hit with the sword.

What is the reason?
It is because he or she has transcended the fear of death.

What percentage of people live well and die well? I would put the number at around 30 percent, and this number likely represents a very outward aspect. The number of people who have died after living a truthful life could be counted on one hand. There are many paintings, yet masterworks can be counted with our fingers. There are countless compositions by musicians, yet truly great pieces are few in number. This does not mean, however, that we can simply give up.

When people live badly and die badly, the reason is typically an excessive fixation on their own lives; they live badly and die badly because of the many diseases and the great anguish that comes about as a result. In the end, living badly is the consequence of making ourselves live badly. What makes us live badly is the desire to possess. The moment that we cast aside that desire is the moment when freedom comes. Our possessions last for only a brief time. In all things, there is nothing that simply remains in its place. It has always been true that things remain for a short time before transforming toward some other place. When we understand the principle of transmission in all things, we can escape the desire to possess. The people who cultivate their lives well are the ones who are effective at managing their minds and bodies, their assets and their affinities. This is what is known as "nurturing life."

When we are capable of shedding our defilements and idle thoughts and transcending fixed ideas through mind-practice, then there will arise in us the wisdom and influential power to keep our mind unaffected inwardly by any difficult things that come while responding appropriately to outward things so that we are not victimized by dangerous things. The tenth section included the Daoist explanation of nurturing life in the form of a question: "Have you cultivated the mind properly and made it gentle like a child through unifying with the Way and disciplining of energy?" The term "nourishing life" could be another way of saying "nurturing life."

The Truth's Profound Grace

The truth gives rise to all things,
Fostering all things with grace.
It gives itself form through objects,
Giving form to its force.

All things respect the truth,
Value and follow its grace.
Elevating the truth and following its grace with respect
Is to become
Without the nature issuing any particular command.

And so, because the truth gives rise to all things,
Because virtue fosters all things,
It disciplines them over the years,
Lingering to make them strong,
Fostering and shielding them.

The truth
Gives rise yet does not possess,
Fosters yet does not depend,
Brings growth yet does not interfere.
This is called the sublime grace of the truth.

This section illuminates the process by which the truth creates and transforms all things in the universe, how this takes place through nonaction and spontaneity, and how the Way expects no compensation despite bestowing this grace.

The principles of the Way provide the principles that create and transform heaven and earth. The virtuous energy of yin and yang nurtures all things. Thus, all things reveal their form initially according to their nature, and all their energy accumulates and they have the power to remain and prosper for some time. Thus the creation and transformation process of spring, summer, fall, and winter takes place not according to some schedule but according to nonaction and spontaneity.

The categories and order are confounded—whether the principle of the Way is the head and virtue what follows, or whether objects are the tail to which the principle of the Way is the head—and they proceed of their own accord.

When humans govern their societies, they do so through the artificial, through action, by establishing policies and all manner of decrees and instructing others to follow them. In contrast, the Way governs heaven and earth and all things through nonaction. From the standpoint of the truth, heaven and earth, and nature, there is no one to give commands, nor anyone to receive them. If we strain to find some human expression for this, it is a matter of respecting the value of the Way and virtue.

Open and Close the Mind's Gateway Properly

The place where the origin of all things lies
Is the matrix of all things under the heaven.
Though we may awaken to that matrix realm,
We must know the providence of all things that is its offspring.

Though we may understand the providence of all things,
We must know how to return to and guard the matrix.
If we do so, there will never be any danger.

Block the hole where it might escape.

Close the door where things enter.
Having done so, do not use it profligately throughout your life.
When you open a hole and contrive sensory things
There will be no deliverance throughout your life.
Clarity, it is said, requires seeing even the subtlest places.
We must know how to guard the soft
Before we are said to be firm.

Though you use light, immediately
Return to the source of brightness.
No disaster will befall your body.
Of this it will be said you have achieved
Justness through mastering the origin.

When practitioners of the Way have awakened through their utmost sincerity to the nameless Way that is the origin and matrix of all things, they must next understand the principles that bear names. Our awakening may only be called complete when we have perceived the original essence and, further, understood the changing principles of all things (the offspring).

Of the people who claim to have practiced the Way, there are many who have understood the stage of voidness that is the essential nature of the truth, but do not understand the phenomenological principles that are the truth's transformations. If we have obtained the no-mind and ever-calm void that is the mind's foundation but remain unaware of the mind's myriad changes to manifest creative transformations, we cannot be said to have understood the mind fully.

The practitioner of the Way performs all actions justly when dealing with objects, but he or she should not forsake the pleasure of returning to the matrix that is the Way's origin and unifying with the stage of no-mind. Though we may venture out into the world and only do things that offer benefit, when we neglect our responsibility to gather experience and cultivate a return to the matrix, we are like the farmer who merely sows and reaps crops in the field without laying manure as fertilizer. Before long, that field will become acidic and crops will not thrive there. To avoid danger, then, the practitioner of the Way must return amid his or her work and strive to sincerely unify with the origin.

Cultivating to return to and unify with the origin is a matter of achieving proper management of the mind, of freely opening and closing the mind's gateway so that when disputes come in from outside, we can close the mind's gateway and keep it from becoming disturbed, deluded, and wrong. At the same time, this process serves to properly purify the various desires that arise in the mind and seek to get out by closing the door tightly so they cannot escape, allowing us to produce and collect states of mind as we wish. If we cultivate ourselves well in this way, there will be no danger; if we do not, there will be no deliverance. The most important concepts for a person driving a car to understand are that they are free to stop and go. Consider how dangerous it is when a driver only knows how to go and does not know how to stop.

Modern people use their brains far more than in the past. Also, we take in countless pieces of information in the Information Age. So if we lose our control because we are not capable of opening and closing our mind's gateway, we become split personalities who are incapable of suppressing our moods and emotions. Almost everyone in the modern era experiences some form of split personality, albeit to differing degrees. It could be said that when a person cannot control the gateway to his or her mind, that person cannot be delivered.

Lecture 53

The Politics of Thieves

If I seek to govern with morals
Because I have understood a little,
I will do so only with a cautious mind.

Great truth is a broad and level road,
Yet people like shortcuts.

The palace is truly clean
Yet the paddies and fields have been left to grow profuse
And the storehouse is empty.

The clothes of the mandarins are beautiful;
They carry sharp swords at their waists.
They eat and drink to surfeit;
Their wealth exists in abundance.

These are the politics of thieves.
They are in great defiance of the politics of morality.

In this section, Laozi considers what he would do if he were to engage in politics. Obviously, he would practice a politics of morality and principles. In practicing politics naturally, he would not run roughshod over his people but proceed carefully, slowly, and appropriately, paying close attention to public opinion. This would seem to be a similar message to recent expressions such as "the public is a lord" and "the customer is king."

People who practice politics poorly leave behind the proper broad and level path of politics in which the public is regarded as a lord. Instead, they follow a darkened path, a crooked path, practicing politics in which the emphasis is on their own state of honor and their attempts to achieve "results" quickly. In other cases, they forget the essence of governance, plundering the people's assets or creating a situation in which the court is wealthy and the people impoverished. The term "thieves" is used as an extreme, deploring way of describing such misguided political leaders.

When people steal things belonging to individuals, we call

them thieves and punish them. The mistaken thoughts, policies, and actions of political leaders cause grave damage to many people and give rise to misfortunes that extend even to the distant future. Thus, we may say that wrongful actions by a political leader represent a thief among thieves.

What Has Been Erected Well Will Not Be Uprooted

What has been erected well will not be uprooted.
What is well embraced will not escape.
Foster your character in this way
And the offerings to posterity will never cease.

Cultivate the truth in yourself
And the grace is true.
Cultivate the truth in the home
And virtue will abound.
Cultivate the truth in the village

And the merits will continue forever.

When a state practices the truth,
Its virtues will abound.
When the truth is practiced across the world
Its grace will spread far and wide.

And so
Unite with character and examine character.
Unite with the home and examine the home.
Become one with the village and examine the village.
Become one with the state and care for the state.
Regard the world as your home and examine the world.
How can I say
That I understand the governance of the world?
There is only the mind-dharma of oneness.

What can be used to tame a person's character? Through study, we come to experience enlightenment and put ideas into practice. But where do we seek to study from? We attempt to learn from friends, from veteran colleagues, from books. When the object of our study is a friend, a veteran colleague, or a book that possesses prejudices, we will become like that person or book as well. The proper way to study is to regard the scriptures of the sages as our textbooks.

The person whose studies cover an even greater breadth and depth learns from the principles of the Way in the universe. The ultimate object of study is the truth that governs the universe.

When we have practiced the Way with our own selves and perfected our character, we will become someone possessed of a truly indestructible character; when we have practiced virtue and embraced our neighbors, this true love will be such that no one can escape its embrace. When a person possesses such a character as a human being, that person will be a sage, earning respect and being honored in ritual by descendants down through the generations.

If people practice morals fully with their whole character, their character will become an avatar of loving-kindness. If they practice morals in the home, abundant virtues will arise in that home. If they strive to practice morals in their village or society or state, this love will spread broadly and without limits.

But what methods do people use in their attempts to govern the home, society, or the state? They try to do so through prejudice, through desire, through honors. Can they ever hope to succeed in such a way?

The way to help the world prosper is not something distant. The principles for governing the body exist within our body. The methods for governing the home, the village, the state and the world do not exist in some book; it is when we become one with that setting and share its rhythms that the miracle remedy for politics can be extracted.

When governance is poor, it is because a gulf exists between the ruler and the ruled. If we bridge that divide, this gap will no longer exist. The more we bridge that divide, the better our governance will be. When we are one, we will be trusted; we will join hands and feel satisfaction in overcoming hardship, no matter what the travails are.

Live like a Newborn

Abundance of grace possessed
Can be likened to a newborn child.

No poisonous insects sting it.
No wild beasts seize it.
No bird of prey claws at it.

Its bones are weak, its muscles soft,
Yet its fist is firm.
It knows not yet of the relations of men and women

Yet its vital energy is whole, its vital power extreme.
It can cry all day and never become hoarse,
Thus it is ultimate harmony.

When we know how to act with harmony, it is called fairness.
When we know fairness, it is called clarity.
When we benefit living creatures, it is called auspicious.
When one mind commands energy, it is called strong.

When we encourage richness in all things, we become decrepit.
This is called poor governance.
If we do not act by the Way and principle, it will wither fast.

When we awaken to the truth and apply it through practice with our body and mind, we are told, the loving-kindness and love will abound, manifesting in the image of a naïve, innocent, and simple child. Laozi compares practice of the Way with various things: with water, with the void, with femininity. Here, he explains it by analogy to a simple, vulnerable child. He seems to show that the Way is the height of loving-kindness, the height of virtue with no mind, and that it is based in a form of giving without signs in which there is no concept whatsoever of compensation.

It is human psychology that we find people difficult to approach when they are too perfect, that we seek to defend ourselves when they are too intelligent, that we dislike them and are not drawn to them when they are excessive. Why is it, then, that all people, when they see a young child, wish to flock to it and give it love, that they show no defenses before it, that they lay down any arms that might attack it? It is because of the pureness, the lack of minds of harm, the vitality and the extreme gentleness. Sages who discipline themselves with the truth come to possess a simple, gentle energy and a spirit of extreme humility, as though they are always wanting. There thus arrives in this a great attractive force drawing others and their neighbors to them, leading them to help in affairs and making them seem like freshly blossoming and un-wilting flowers.

There are times when we must receive things we do not wish to receive. There are no more awkward times than these. At such times, we feel insulted even when we give. This is a foolish action, lacking perspective and showing a desire to show off our giving to others. The wise person knows to pay close attention to what others need and to give exactly what they need. After giving, they feel no mind of boasting. Their actions become upstanding virtue and auspicious behavior.

From our childhood, we are well acquainted with the story of the Wind and the Sun. No cold or rough winds could make the passing man take off his coat, but the gentle and warm sunshine led the traveler to remove it. In this way, the violent approach to governance and way to live will wither and fail before long, however much it may seem to be successful at the time. It is the loving-kindness that abounds in warmth that represents wisdom, the auspicious thing that will inspire admiration in the minds of others so that they will be well governed and join your side, making you an eternally strong person.

The Person Who Truly Understands Does Not Speak

The person who truly understands does not speak.
Those who speak often cannot be said to understand well.

Block the door that emanates vital energy.
Close the door of temptation.
Make blunt the sharp discriminations.
Organize the fragmented knowledge.

When we harmonize the light of our wisdom
With the secular world,

We are said to have unified with the sublimeness of the truth.

Such a person
Is not especially more familiar with things
Nor more distant,
Nor does he or she regard them as beneficial,
Nor does he or she do harm,
Nor does he or she prize them,
Nor does he or she regard them as mean.

And so
The person who has unified with the truth
Will be regarded as noble in the world.

When we awaken to and understand the fundamental principles of the universe, we understand that the wholesome and unwholesome share the same origin. And because we fully understand the thing that makes all things, including the wholesome and unwholesome, such that they cannot be otherwise, we do not speak needless words but focus on practicing with ourselves. The person who does not understand well or who understands only partially will make many excuses and say many things that are more beneficial not said.

People who awaken to the Way and put it into practice can adjust and use their knowledge, yet that knowledge does not lose its humanity or do harm to ethics or morality. It is good when we can use a knife or fire properly, but consider the great harm that they can do when used poorly. We must understand that it is the same with knowledge: it can be very good when used well, but when it is used poorly the damage can be very serious. When we establish ourselves well as moral actors and command knowledge, we must not become slaves to knowledge and lose our humanity. It has sometimes been said in recent years that advanced education makes us inhuman. The more formal education we have, we are told, the more undutiful and arrogant we become.

It is difficult to constrain the character or define the character of the person who has awakened to the truth and puts it into practice as any one thing. He or she seems gentle yet rigid, high yet low, low yet aloof, as hard-working as a host yet as disinterested as a guest. All of these may be described as the advanced ability to act in the right way for every moment and every situation.

The practitioner of the Way is someone who performs the proper buddha offerings and acts timely, working appropriately for every situation and every person encountered. He or she is someone with the loving capabilities to face any person appropriately, kind or wicked, and only make that person better than he or she is now.

This Is How to Govern a Country

The governance of a country must follow the right Way.
Military operations must be conducted cleverly
Yet all must be approached through nonaction.
How can I know such a thing?
All the sages have said so.

When a country shuns and bans many things
The people become more impoverished.
When the people possess the many conveniences of civilization
A civilization becomes more chaotic.

When people's tactics are numerous
Many undesirable things will arise.
The more laws there are in a country
The more thieves will arise there.

And so the sage says
If I behave in accordance with morals,
The people will be edified of their own accord.
If I appreciate tranquility
The people will become proper of their own accord.
If few things happen that are without use
The people will prosper.
If I have no desires
The people will be simple.

Governance of a country must be conducted in accordance with the proper way, and although one may be forced to conduct matters in abnormal ways following military tactics during wartime, those two things must be grounded in moral politics if one is to attain all there is under heaven.

Where weapons are numerous, national strength is wasted on the production of weapons of war and the people are forced to endure poverty, leading to confusion in spiritual values because of the pursuit of armed forces and material values. When the law develops, this only results in the proliferation of schemes to evade the law, which cannot be good for the education of the public.

A political leader's personality, values, and philosophy are immediately evident in the way he or she runs the country. When the divide deepens between a leader and the public, the former is forced to use his or her authority and violence to rule. The person who possesses philosophy, firmly convinced of the goodness and morality within the mind-nature of human beings, will adopt a different form of politics.

The politics of the sage is a matter of leaving things to spontaneity when possible, of obeying the principles so that governance does not interfere too much in people's lives, of governing morally through nonaction to bolster the self-reliance, autonomy, and self-purifying capabilities of the people.

When our bodies are wounded, they will heal themselves over time with a minimum amount of treatment. When we tamper too much trying to heal them, the wounds last longer, leading over time to different diseases emerging as the body's self-reliance is weakened. Similarly, those who strive excessively to establish morality and regulate people with the law in governing a country may seem successful for a while, but will come to sacrifice their autonomy over time.

When Politics Is Magnanimous

When a government is magnanimous
The people become simple.
When a government scrutinizes too much
The people become confused and wander.
Oh, disaster! It is a parasite on happiness.
Oh, happiness! It lies hidden within disaster.

All must know how to change,
When happiness and disaster are at their most extreme.
All must know that there is no rightness in the extreme.

The right is prone to changing to the strange,
The kind to the wicked.
People are foolish.
That foolishness is eternity.

And so the sage
Does not cut, though he or she is clear,
Does not spoil, though he or she is clean,
Is straight, yet is not rude,
Shines, yet does not flutter.

When a political leader governs generally, in broad strokes, the people will naturally become free and simple. When the leader scrutinizes too much in the hopes of "succeeding," he or she will demand that people do better, discovering mistakes and attempting to correct them as the people grow more disgruntled. It is the providence of nature, however, that disasters arise even amid success as a result of flaws. The principle of the universe is such that things reverse direction when they reach an extreme. When they hit an extreme, they change. So we are told that the path to good governance of a country lies in realizing this and adopting a non-interventionist approach in which the public is guided to follow their discretion.

Because sages have mastered the principle by which wholesomeness, unwholesomeness, happiness and misfortune cycle, they distinguish clearly between wholesome and unwholesome but do not merely cut away things that are mistaken; they are upright, yet do not use that integrity to cause excessive wounds to the turbid; they clearly possess shining achievements and wisdom, yet they strive to avoid provoking or hurting incompetent people by revealing them.

Even when sages are making clear distinctions and judgment, they may appear unsophisticated, unfocused, and inconsistent in the eyes of others. Yet in the end all things are revealed to be perfect, and they embrace all things and enable leadership to occur as people understand themselves.

In scrutinizing things too closely, we are trying to make things pleasant, but this can actually result in more problems. There are also times when being "lazy" and merely observing a situation results in a problem dying away. Happiness and misfortune are always closely tied together. We must understand this principle: when happiness becomes too much, we suffer misfortune, and when misfortune is severe, we adopt a new sense of resolution and create happiness. Thus, doing well does not guarantee that all things will succeed. Sometimes scratching an itch will only make things worse. This happens because we do not fully understand the principle behind the prosperity and degeneration of things.

Deep Roots and a Sturdy Stalk

In governing people and serving the truth,
There is nothing better than economy.

Typically, when we conserve our spirit,
We return easily to the original nature.
When we return to the original nature, great grace accumulates;

When great grace accumulates
There is nothing we cannot overcome.
And so if there is nothing that is amiss

The road ahead is endless.

Such a person is capable of taking charge of a country.
If such a person is the matrix of the state,
That state's future is eternal.

This is called depth of root and firmness of stalk.
It refers to the Way and is a principle that lets us live long and see
   forever.

A great leader knows how to be scrupulously stinting, as he or she is more reserved when it comes to his or her passion and spirit. That which is held back in terms of spiritual ability must be allowed to cluster and build within so that spiritual ability is strengthened with one mind. A mind that is scattered cannot display any strength, but when we gather it well we acquire the attractive power to make a deep impression on people and lead the public. It is a mysterious strength by which things are accomplished without action, simply through aspiration of the mind.

Physical strength too must be mustered to produce great force. An organization must be united to show great strength. This is all the more time for the spirit, which displays a fearsome ability to lead when united. People today, however, are constantly listening, looking, thinking, and acting without rest, so that they have no leisure for their clean and pure one-pointedness to come together and unite. This has resulted in many modern people with split personalities whose spirits are divided, causing them to lose self-control.

If we wish to become leaders, we must know how to conserve and gather our spirit for use. The person with great power that arises from gathering the spirit has the wisdom, resolve, and courage to handle all the different affairs of the state. Such political leaders are worthy of being entrusted with the nation.

Governing a Country Is like Cooking a Tiny Fish

In governing a large country
We must act as though carefully cooking a tiny fish.
If we govern by this principle of the Way,
Even ghosts cannot use their powers.

Not only do ghosts not use their powers
But spirits cannot harm humans.
Not only will spirits not harm humans
But even politicians cannot harm their public.
As we help one another,
Virtue returns to the sage and citizens.

Ordinary political leaders represent the interests of their associates or succumb to a design to show off with their politics or make excessive efforts to reflect their ideals in the reality of politics. None of these approaches is desirable.

Here, we are told that a leader running a country must conduct politics with the greatest of care, just as a cook preparing a tiny, young fish must exercise great care to preserve its form.

The leader must pay close attention to the public's emotional state and act in a way that suits it. Typically, political leaders handle their affairs in a self-centered way, making themselves the focus of their policy decisions. When this results in behaviors that defy public opinion, the leader's governance will ultimately fail.

If a leader conducts politics in a magnanimous and vigorous way, surveying the public's feelings closely and creating policies centered on the public so that the public follows of its own accord without the leader focusing too much on implementation or the people having to trust too much in the state, then what power does another politician—or even a ghost—have to harm those people?

In the past, peoples and societies suffered from rather superstitious phenomena, and ghosts often interfered in people's lives. The village shrines that remain today and the customs for driving out ghosts or for summoning and serving them are all signs of the extent to which societies suffered at the hands of superstitions and spirits. The message here, however, is that when a political leader conducts politics of nonaction, the people and society as a whole will join together and transform with right energy so that these superstitions do little to hurt people's lives, and no ambitious politicians can deceive that society.

The Great Country like the River's Lower Course

The great country is like the river's lower course.
The river's end is where all the waters converge.
It is like the males of the world
Congregating with the females.

Femininity, being tranquil,
Always defeats masculinity
And exists always beneath in its tranquility.

The great country, with humility toward smaller countries,

Wins the minds of the small countries.
The small country, with humility toward the great country,
Wins the minds of the large country.

The great country gains through lowering;
The small country too gains through lowering;
Both gain through humility.

The great country merely loves
To govern over people;
The small country merely loves to go beneath people
And serve.

The large and small country
Obtain what they wish to obtain from each other.
How great are the merits of humility!

If we look at natural phenomena, we see that low depressions become filled over the years, while high peaks are cut down with time. That is nature. When something exists in a low state over a long period of time, crustal movements lift it up. This is the alternating predominance of yin and yang that governs nature, the principle by which yin becomes yang when it reaches an extreme and yang becomes yin when it reaches an extreme. When a big country interacts with a small one, eternal peace comes when their diplomacy is one of mutual modesty and humility. What happens when something seems to be elevated in defiance of the principles of nature? Just as the mountaintop is lowered over the years, or the tall tree is bowed by the wind, so the artificially elevated thing will be cut down.

Laozi discusses a governance of lowering, or a politics of waiting, as methods of living in this world and conducting political affairs. Considering the diplomatic frictions between the countries of the world today, I think that he is offering an approach to diplomacy that he feels big and small countries should adopt with one another. Perhaps we should consider a political approach of comfortably waiting for others to act on their own, working with them from behind as much as possible instead of leading from ahead.

Valuable Words Sell Quickly

Truth is a deep place in all things.
It is the jewel of the kind person
And lies hidden even in those who are not kind.

Valuable words sell quickly.
Lofty actions are models for people.
How can we abandon things for not being nice?

To enthrone an emperor in the world
And serve the three ministers,

We seek to greet them in pomp with jewels and four-horse carts,
Yet it is more important still
To sit and teach the truth.

Why has the truth been regarded as so precious since long ago?
The person who has obtained the truth
Gains without seeking
And can break free of whatever transgressions he or she commits.
That is why the truth is regarded as so precious.

Working externally to establish the true mind is the role of education and politics, while teaching the true mind directly and helping others to make it a part of their lives internally is the role of religion. This passage is a clear illustration of how the edifying activities of religion must take precedence over the political.

Kind people and unkind people alike possess a true mind hidden deep within them. The noble goal of living is to discover this mind and to practice it in one's daily life without losing sight of it.

The pursuit of material things and external honors is merely an embellishment. Working externally to establish the true mind is the role of education and politics, while teaching the true mind directly and helping others to make it part of their lives internally is the role of religion.

Sage figures who possess capability in religion will be encouraged to go into politics. If they do go into politics, they will bring benefits to real-world political dealings. But it is of far more value in terms of promoting human morality and creating a moral society for sages to engage in religious edification activities, even if others may disregard them to some extent.

Through the Spontaneity That
Does without Doing

Through the spontaneity that does without doing,
Though we work, we do so by the principles;
Though we taste, there is no binding to the taste.

Through the small, achieving the great;
Through the few, assembling many things.
Resentment is repaid with virtue.

Difficult things are sought first through the simple;
Great things are grown from the very small.

All difficult things under heaven
Arise perforce from the simple.
The great things of the world
Are formed from tiny actions.

The sage, because he or she does not think of him- or herself as great,
Can ably achieve great things.
That which grants permissions casually and loosely
Is perforce lacking in faith.
When many things are simple
Difficulties are necessarily lurking.

And so the sage always views things as difficult,
Working with great care
Until finally nothing is difficult.

This section offers an answer to the question of what capabilities the sage possesses. Ordinary practitioners of the Way may seem unaware of the ways of the world, yet we recognize them as kindhearted people; such people are third- and fourth-class practitioners. Practitioners who have disciplined themselves with the truth are people possessed of tremendous capabilities.

Such people seem to live comfortably because they do not lose their tranquility, acting with a state of mind that seems to do without doing, which makes them appear slow and deliberate to those around them. They are effective at measuring the starting points, the process, the conclusions, and the ripple effects of actions, preparing in advance and examining all necessary things. Thus, we should label this stage as that of a master of his or her affairs.

All things in the world progress gradually and incrementally. Ordinary people fail to read the direction in which things are gradually and incrementally progressing, only to be astonished at the big result that manifests. The hidden, unseen causes in affairs do not go away; they grow, building toward some outcome. These outcomes then begin anew in various ways, scattering and concealing themselves again. It is similar to the way in which we sow seeds in spring, nurturing them to lush profusion in the summer so that they bear fruit in the fall. When the winter comes, we move those fruits and store them in different places, and their seeds go on to greet the next spring. Only by practicing to properly interpret this foundation, process, and result can we become great workers.

People live their lives in relationship of exchange. Ordinary people seek to take much from others while giving little. We say that such people lack a conscience, but almost all of us adopt this way of thinking in our lives. The conscientious person seeks to give as much as he or she receives and to receive as much as he or she gives. If we consider this to be a horizontal relationship, then the person at an advanced level, the level of the sage, seeks to give much while receiving little. We ought to consider which kind of person we are.

Some cases of exchange involve the trading of resentment. Ordinarily, we seek to retaliate when we suffer some grievance. People at a different level forgive others even when they are bad. The person filled with the sage's mind of loving-kindness transcends mere forgiveness after suffering harm; instead, he or she becomes one who practices the greatest grace and greatest virtue by embracing and giving love.

There may be times, however, when we punish someone because they do harm repeatedly, we feel that their habit can only be changed through remonstration and punishment rather than repaid in virtue, or there is some educational value in punishing them in light of the social climate. But we must not overlook the fact that the mind-set of the advanced person who disciplines necessarily carries a profound love and desire to teach.

Sages remain forever in an incomplete state. Having contemplated the principle by which the moon wanes once it becomes full and the flower withers after reaching full blossom, sages carry within them many possibilities at all times, yet they refuse to be defined as complete. We should take great heed of and learn from this mind-dharma of the sages.

Sages seem to have the habit of starting everything with difficulty and conducting their affairs carefully. I believe this is because errors are prone to happen when ordinary people are too confident and haughty, and mistakes follow when we regard others lightly.

Sages Do Not Act Out of Desire

The stable is easily sustained;

When there are no signs, it is easy to plan.

The frail is easily shattered;

Weak things are prone to scattering.

Take measures before the signs emerge.

Treat it before there is disorder.

The great branching tree came from a tiny sprout.

The soaring tower was built from piles of grains.

The thousand-*li* journey begins with a single step.

He or she who seeks to win will likely lose.

He or she who fixates will likely let things slip.
The sage, not doing, does not lose through doing;
Not fixating, he or she does not let things slip.

If we examine how ordinary people work,
They always lose around the time they might succeed.
If we are as attentive to the end as we are to the beginning
We will succeed in all things.

And so the sage
Does not work out of desire,
Does not value material things that are difficult to obtain.
He or she studies the truth that others do not study,
Returns to the truth other people have passed by.
Though he or she helps all things through spontaneity,
He or she does not dare defy spontaneity with the artificial.

Ordinary people become attached to and come to prefer things that are large and numerous. People these days go to the florist and buy flowers that have already blossomed, and then they merely look at them. As a result, they know nothing of the beginning or process behind the flowering. Yet how is it that the big, the numerous, the distant becomes complete? We must understand the great value of beginnings and that which is small in number.

One might say that the wise person is the one who does not

become attached to or crave an outcome but who instead focuses on the sincerity that goes into the beginning and creation of a final product.

People who insist only on winning or who become too attached to possessions cause themselves grave suffering. They also cause suffering to those around them. In general, all things, human minds, and even the people suffering from attachment are constantly changing and in flux. Nothing simply exists at any given moment; everything is transforming, changing locations, and existing in flux. No one can stop that flow because it flows by the power of the truth. We must realize that the possessions that we have now have only been given to us for a certain amount of time.

The cause of failure lies in racing too hastily, in becoming drunk with arrogance, in being lazy and neglectful and thus lacking in heedfulness. There is a Korean expression that warns against this, likening such recklessness to "sinking your snot in finished rice." When something is processing toward completion, we must be very cautious about acting without heedfulness, lest we spoil our work with a slight mistake.

When conducting affairs, we are told that sages do not act out of desire; they do so according to the principles of the Way, and they do not become attached to the material. This is due to all of the spiritual effort it consumes to manage and preserve material things once we possess them, and it is done so that sages can commit their energies to the mind-practice and practice with the study of the Way that others do not study. It also enables them to focus fully on the cultivation to find and restore the realm of truth that people overlook—the original nature of the mind.

Today is the dawn of the age of the sage. Others may have succeeded somewhat and advanced in the world through injustice with desire and arms, but in the coming age nothing that is unjust will succeed. It will be an age when we must prosper together with others, and when success will eternally elude us if we lack philosophy. We must begin our efforts to become sages.

The Person of Good Moral Practice

Those who engage in good moral practice in the olden days
Did not merely seek to educate the public
And make them smart
But disciplined them in
Simple humanity.

When a country is difficult to govern
It is because there are many people there who merely know.
When we govern a country merely through knowledge
We become a thief to that country.

To govern instead through simplicity
Becomes a blessing to that country.

Knowing these two things,
We must set the frame for ruling a nation.
The person who does well in establishing regulations to rule a nation
Is said to possess the virtue of the truth.
Oh, virtue of the truth! It is deep and eternal.
This is the opposite of the ways of the world
Yet it leads to a reign of peace.

Today, just as it was in ancient times, education that merely involves acquiring knowledge and techniques has always been a mistaken endeavor. True education is education that allows us to practice humanity. Lately, many have talked about how those with advanced education become inhumane. It ought to be the case that people with more education have greater human feeling and a more morally noble character. Yet many have become selfish, complacent, calculating, and immoral people because their focus has been on education in knowledge and ability, without valuing the practice of pure humanity. A country whose education centered on knowledge and ability in this way may appear to develop outwardly, but its people's spirits will degenerate.

There will be some true benefit to people's lives in the powerful economy where the people's spirits have degenerated. When these spirits become immoral in the distant future, all of this external prosperity will ultimately come crashing down.

True education is not a matter of making the public ignorant. A country will only be blessed when its education is focused less on knowledge and more on the practice of restoring morality, when it fosters a sense of ownership and values pure humanity, and when it is built with such people serving as its elite.

The Sage Does Not Burden Others

The river and sea are the better of the hundred valleys
Because they lie beneath them.
Thus, they are ably kings of the hundred valleys.

If the sage wishes to go before the public,
he or she must engage in humble words and deeds.
If the sage wishes to go before the public
He or she must necessarily place ourselves behind.

Though the sage exists above the people,

The people do not see it as a burden.
Though he or she may stand before them and lead
The people do not resent it.
They cheerfully vote for the sage
And never despise him or her.

Because the sage gains without competing,
There is no one in this world who can compete.

This section once again explains the mind-dharma of the sage, who leads through the principles with the virtue of humility and the virtue of noncompetition. Sages possess a full range of skills, with unlimited wisdom and virtue and decision-making ability, yet they also strive to always study and nurture virtue under others. Even when they find themselves forced to stand before others and work as a leader, they work amid a climate in which others gladly choose them, and so they are able to fulfill their role as a leader within the principles. This represents an advanced level of capability.

Rather than stepping forward personally to lead, sages seek to realize their ideals through others. Why should that be? It may be because practical politics involves such a complex tangle of interests, causing people to become swept into unnecessary disputes and creating obstacles to practice of the Way, and yet at the same time they wish to give joy to others who wish to engage in politics.

Ordinary leaders exhaust their energies being conscious of rivals in their actions and trying to eliminate foes. As a result, their political aspirations are doomed to fail. Sages are superior first and foremost because they have no rivals, and so they are not conscious of others. The sage thus regards him- or herself as his or her own greatest enemy and does not neglect to cultivate him- or herself morally. As such, they become leader-caliber figures and serve as a standard by which others measure themselves.

Laozi's Three Jewels

The people of the world all say
The truth I have illuminated
Is too great
And thus does not seem bright.

Generally, things that are too large
Do not appear wise.
If I were fixed with wisdom,
I would have been a small person long ago.

In my possession are three jewels.

Even now, I commit the sincerest efforts to guarding and preserving
them well.

The first is loving-kindness;

The second is thrift;

The third is not standing before others.

Because of loving-kindness, I can ably be brave;

Because of thrift, I can ably broaden;

Because I do not stand in front,

I can be first in the world.

If one is brave without loving-kindness,

If one broadens without thrift,

If one seeks to let go of standing behind and take the lead,

He or she will end in annihilation.

Fight with loving-kind mind and you will win.

Guard with loving-kindness and you will be strong.

Heaven will aid such a person

And guard him or her with loving-kindness.

Ordinary people regard material things as jewels. Slightly better
people regard techniques as jewels. They also place value on affinities. To the sage, the jewel is the mind-dharma, or the dharma
of using the mind, which is obtained through exercising discipline
with the truth. We ought to consider carefully just what we regard

as the most important jewels. Material things and visible phenomena are bound to transform and disappear. Techniques and knowledge constantly change and advance, so that we fall behind if we do not work all the time to attain something higher and deeper. If we do fall behind, everything becomes terribly futile. All things come and go according to the mind. The dharma of using the state of mind that is obtained through truthful discipline can be used as long as we exist and can be respected eternally because it is truthful.

For example, it is far better to teach people the method for making bread than to give them lots of bread. But more important than the skill of making bread is the fair mind that knows to distribute bread equitably.

The mind of loving-kindness is love without condition and virtue without ostentation. When we possess such love, there will emerge the kind of courage where we would die for those we love. Admiral Yi Sun-sin's spirit of love for his country gave rise to the courage of the commoner fighters; so, too, with the forgiving spirit of Gandhi and the spirit of loving-kindness in all the sages. But courage and determination without loving-kindness are reckless and can produce actions that are of no value to others or to oneself.

"Frugality" is a term that refers to sparingness in the spirit and material things; when we are frugal, things will accumulate, and that accumulation allows us to then broaden our virtuous edification. These are the principles. To seek to broaden without having accumulated is not within the principles. Instead, it leaves us piled with debt, causing us to fail. And because there is no spiritual accumulation, it brings about devastation of the spirit.

When we place others first, we necessarily come next. Opportunities will come as a matter of course when we accumulate virtue and build our strength, putting others first and helping them. In the process, we become strong leaders who move forward while helping and conceding to many others.

Conversely, those who proceed by force and by breaking others down will not stay in the lead for long before they collapse.

Ability without Discord

The scholar with ability
Does not use weapons.
The general who fights well
Does not rise in anger.

The general who vanquishes foes
Never confronts them.
The person who commands others well is humble.
This is called virtue without discord;
It is called the capability of commanding people.

Because such a person can be compared with heaven,
It has long been said that his or her capability has reached the ultimate.

The most successful general is the general who wins without a battle; the most capable person is the one who succeeds in his or her affairs through virtuous edification. The person who succeeds in fighting is only slightly better off than his or her opponent. It is a matter of who is the slightly bigger acorn. So what must we do to win without fighting? When a person has made ample preparations in advance and acquired great virtuous edification, the enemy will not want to fight because he or she does not stand a chance.

We have many elections today, and sometimes the candidates are neck and neck. Other times, they give only the appearance of a contest when everyone already knows what the outcome will be. In some cases, a candidate will win without a vote. When we observe the foundation of what we would do and make many investments in advance to become thoroughly prepared, and when we acquire much virtuous edification, we will be capable of winning through transcending our rival and through concession. Such a leader is the greatest leader of all.

What is the biggest secret to managing and commanding others? It may work for us to give many rewards, we are told, but it is through understanding and respecting others that we inspire them to full and passionate loyalty. People, we are told, will seek to follow those who notice numerous strengths in others and draw on them at timely moments—that is, those who use the gifts of others as their own. This is humility in the broadest sense.

An Age-Old Message to the Soldier

There is something that has long been recommended to soldiers:
Do not fixate on fighting
And become the prime actor;
Observe objectively, like a guest;
Be more prepared for great retreats
Than winning small victories with advancements.

This is going without leaving a trace.
Though we repel, we use not our arms.
We grasp without the use of weapons.

Though we try to grasp, there is no enemy soldier.

There is no greater disaster
Than contempt for your foe.
View your foe lightly
And your fortune will be lost.
When soldiers fight together in similar ways
It is the ones who grieve who are said to triumph.

When we become too attached to our affairs or allow our emotions to take precedence, we typically make errors in our judgment and cause those affairs to go awry. Whether at war or in competition, our chances of winning are high when we work with a sense of conviction while acting like a bystander, like someone kibitzing from a third-party perspective on a game of chess or Go. If we are capable of objectively observing the battlefield in war with a state of mind of leisure and magnanimity, we may be able to grasp the distribution of enemy forces, the soldiers' morale, or the character of the enemy general. If we also have a firm understanding of our own side's capabilities as we wage war, victory should not be difficult.

The basic attitude toward war here is that the person who possesses human love and the mind of loving-kindness will ultimately win. The aim of war, in the end, is to fight for the sake of humanity. The person who wages war to show off military might, to seize riches, to avenge wrongdoing, or to broaden territory will finally be ensnared by the battlefield and will inevitably attempt reckless operations because of unwise desires and the hope of winning. The person who has the mind of loving-kindness and love for humanity, however, is possessed of wisdom and courage and determination; it is that person, we are told, who is capable of the ultimate victory in war. This is a section that demands deep consideration.

It is far wiser to prepare to consider the overall situation and prepare so that we can achieve surrender without fighting than to pursue small, immediate gains. While progress is important to the person who has become a general, it is also important to prepare for a retreat. In short, one can become a true victor not by fighting and winning but by building one's abilities to encourage the other to surrender without any thought of fighting.

The Sage Dressed in Reeds and Holding Jade to His Breast

My words are profoundly easy to understand,
Profoundly simple to put into practice.
Yet the people of the world
Neither understand nor practice them.

Words have a head;
Work has a center.
How should they know me
If they do not know this?

Rare are those who truly understand me;

Precious are those who emulate me.

And so they should say of the sage, wearing clothes of reeds,

That he or she seems to hold jade to his or her bosom.

The people of the world are all too busy in their attachments to their lives here and now, and they seem to not know where they are headed at this moment. Each day of our life here and now is proceeding toward death, yet instead of recognizing death, we are focused on the problems of living today. How could people who live such lives listen to the words of the truth, words that are fundamental and macroscopic, words that are easy to understand and would not be difficult at all to put into practice if one merely took an interest? Today, as in the ancient past, such a person seems to be truly rare.

The words of the sages necessarily have parts that form their cardinal doctrine. There are parts that constitute the principles of the universe. Their words are necessarily based in the truth as they are presented.

Just as attorneys base their arguments in the law, so the words of sages are presented in such a way that the truth is their foundation. If a religion is not based in the truth in this way, it is not a religion but more of a social group. If it does claim to be a religion, it is merely a pseudo-faith.

As we go about our affairs, there is a goal that we must regard as fundamental. When we are governing a country or teaching students, there is some element that constitutes the substance of our actions. If we lose sight of this, then what we do is not work but the disruption of work.

It is something like the police officer who is tasked with maintaining peace and order in a country but who destroys social order as he or she goes about his or her duties. Laozi teaches that we must understand the essence of work as we approach it and bring this essence into being.

Sages do the thing that is the most necessary for people, yet they may have been fated to have others disregard them.

Confucius said that when engaged in edification, he was like a dog at a home in mourning. Jesus was rewarded by being nailed to a cross by the Jewish people.

The Sage Never Sickens

Knowing, yet seeming to not know.
If unceasing in one's studies
Is said to be supreme;
Then thinking that one understands when one does not
Is a sickness of wisdom.

Generally, there may be treatment for disease
When we regard it as a disease.

The sage never sickens.

Because he or she regards disease as disease,
He or she cannot fall ill.

People who never understand and people who stop learning because they believe they understand are always foolish people. But people who never understand are humble because they are aware that they do not really understand, and so they do not commit transgressions. People who are confident that they understand, in contrast, are actually not aware, yet they teach others as though they understand what they have not awakened to or understand incorrectly. As a result, they are a type of people who commit grave transgressions and suffer from serious sickness.

Sages understand, yet they constantly pursue new learning and hone what they have learned to know more accurately, to know more broadly, to know fundamentally, to understand even the things that change over time. So they are always humble and seeking to study, and so they speak placidly without defining things as one thing or another.

Sages possess truly great intellectual desire and discipline with wisdom, and they never stop learning or neglect to teach, for teaching is a way of studying well. Furthermore, they analyze everything and continue to contemplate intuitively, shining the lantern of wisdom.

Choosing the Real and Forsaking the False

If the people do not regard the majesty of the king
As an object of fear,
That king will possess great and true majesty.

If a king does not seek to suppress the lives of his subjects,
Those subjects will not despise their king.
Generally, where there is no mind of dislike
The other does not dislike us either.

The sage,

In knowing himself or herself,

Does not vaunt his or her abilities,

In loving himself or herself,

Does not seek to be treated as noble.

And so he or she chooses the substantial

And forsakes ostentation.

The fear and nervousness that lower-ranking people feel as they sit before the ceremonial grandeur of someone higher is evidence that the relationship between high and low in that group is one of distrust. A truly mature high-low relationship is one that accepts the principles that both sides must observe, yet where the lower person knows how to break free of form when addressing the person higher up. As such, when we lead an organization in this way, there will emerge a true form of grandeur, one where every member in the organization gives his or her trust and there is absolute confidence to support it. The leader's words will be followed by absolute obedience rooted in the trust of all members. This is the meaning of fundamental dignity.

There have been several different interpretations of this section, but I view the message as meaning that sages, while aware of their capabilities, do not let this show. Moreover, despite the fact that they exhibit love for themselves, they do not seek to be treated with substanceless estimation by others. Thus, I see it as meaning that the most desirable form of power is one based in true respect that arises from a loving high-low relationship where there is no fear of formal power.

Humans have residences, and they have the domains of their lives. To restrict those domains is to infringe upon freedom, which is the limitation that human beings hate the most. An exciting politics is a politics that does not infringe upon freedom.

The Net of Truth Is Loose, but One Cannot Escape It

One may die because of bold resolution.
One may live by acting with caution.

Bravery and caution are both beneficial and harmful.
Who can understand the reason
The truth hates and punishes?
And so the sage
Handles affairs with caution.

The way the truth governs all things

Is by winning with fighting,
Responding well without words,
Making things come without calling,
Planning well in silence.

The net of truth is broad, very broad and loose,
Yet nothing escapes it.

Consider history, your neighbors, or the various affairs of the world. We call them good when they are bold, but that boldness brings its share of error. A cautious attitude is said to be better than youthful courage, but there are cases where affairs are handled mistakenly because of caution. In terms of statistics, all of these things are difficult to declare as sound decisions or beneficial actions. No matter how we try to survey the reality or how we distinguish the causes behind the benefit and harm or gains and losses there, it is impossible to distinguish them all. As such, the sage first engages in the work of awakening to the truth. He or she also considers and studies what the optimal method is, considering things heedfully as he or she handles his or her affairs. As a result, he or she always succeeds.

It is said that rightness always wins in the end. Some take this to mean that things necessarily return to the way they were destined to be. Who can know this destiny? What exists to foreordain matters? This, we are told, is the Way. And so the sage becomes a seeker of the Way. He or she contemplates the outcomes of affairs. He or she always approaches matters carefully in handling them. One does not know where the truth lies. One does not know how it observes the affairs of people. The net of this truth is loosely woven, yet we cannot escape this net. Whenever anyone transgresses, the Way remembers it and punishes it; when people do good things, it remembers all and gives happiness. How could we ever deceive the Way?

There are times in society when the people who are denounced are the ones who prosper and bask in their lives. Conversely, there are also situations where those who people wish for a long life suffer misfortune. Viewed in these real-world terms, matters seem unfair. How should we understand these phenomena? Who is the entity that creates these fates, these destinies? It is the theory of karma: We are receiving what we ourselves created. We have no way of knowing what karma we created in past lives. We must live heedfully and do the right things in terms of justice and morality.

The Truth Is What Punishes

When the people do not fear death
How can we threaten them with killing?

If the people were made
To regard death always with fear
And commit immoral acts,
Such a leader
Would wish to kill the people.

Yet who would dare to kill them?

For there is a truth of its own
That ever makes us kill those who would kill.

To kill when it is not your responsibility
Is like a person felling a tree for a lumberjack:
Rare is the one who will not injure his or her hands.

In the governance of a nation or organization, there are times when the people or members become tired of a leader's tyranny. When they reach this rough state of mind, they fear nothing. No methods work when matters degenerate to this state. The people will wish to kill the leader, and they will do so. What we are told here, however, is that it is not right for someone to kill a corrupt leader and claim that it is righteous to do so.

Presiding over the universe is a truth that will punish the transgressions we commit. The wise course, then, is for us to know how to clearly distinguish between what humans must do and what the truth must do. When we ourselves perform the punishment that is the truth's to deal out, another person will come forward and repeat the same thing. We can see this in the frequent revolutions that occur in places such as the world's underdeveloped countries

In practical terms, we cannot deal punishment ourselves when the people next to us do bad things. We must notify the authorities, and the authority will determine the severity of the crime and assign a suitable punishment. In the same way, there are cases where people attempt to assassinate or otherwise harm a national leader that they view as having done wrong. This, however, cannot be a rightful action. The punishment of human transgressions and rewarding of good deeds is ultimately up to the truth of the universe to perform, and humans should not attempt to intervene. We must distinguish, we are told, between the work of humans and what is the truth's to decide.

The People Left Starving by Excessive Taxes

When the people starve
It is typically because leaders collect too many taxes.
Thus it is that the people starve.

When the people are difficult to govern
It is because their leaders govern by force.
Thus, they are not governed.

When the people take a light view of death
It is because their leaders live in abundance.

Thus, the people take a light view of death.

Political leaders must live only with the empty mind
This is the wise path of regarding life as precious.

When a country's population is poor and difficult to rule—so much so that the citizens think nothing of death—the blame lies purely with the people practicing politics there. When political leaders live lavishly while collecting excessive taxes and handling the people with force, that nation is in grave jeopardy. It is a serious matter for the public when the country is imperiled or collapses, but it is more fatal still for the leaders. Leaders must therefore change their approach to living; there is no other way. They must govern purely through nonaction, and they must also govern through nondesire. The wise way to achieve this, we are told, is for the people to survive, for the country to be safe, and for the political leaders themselves to value life.

First, political leaders must help their people avoid poverty. To do so, they should collect taxes that are fair, just, and proper, ensuring that the public's will is not drained. Those taxes must then be used for the public's sake. Second, the country must be governed in a reasonable, spontaneous way, rather than through intrigues and violence, so that the public plays a part in national policies and the country is run without problems. Third, the leaders and privileged classes must not pursue their interests alone.

What sort of character will the needy develop when the gap between the rich and poor grows too great? These people will risk their own lives rebelling.

The important thing for a political leader to do, this section tells us, is to collect taxes fairly, to govern by the principles and spontaneity, and to have a mind-set of honest poverty.

Softness Is the Essence of Life

The life force of people
Is replete when it is soft and fragile.
The content of death is rigid and strong.

All things and plants are soft and tender when living,
Dry and stiff when dead.
And so the firm and strong are the followers of death.
The frail are the followers of life.

If a country focuses on having a strong military

It will eventually fail to win and collapse.
The tree that is rigid is felled,
The strong falls down,
The frail rises up.

Look at the bodies of infants and children. How frail and soft they are! Now look at the body of an old man. How stiff and rigid! Yet the softness of the child faithfully weaves together life, while the rigid body of the old man urges death onward.

Look closely at a tree. Notice that the soft stems are above, while the rigid stem is below. Yet these two are merely phenomena. The softness of water bores through the hardness of the rock as it eddies against it. Let us think deeply about these natural phenomena. The person who adopts nature as a textbook and learns from it can be described as a sage, a practitioner of the Way, a master of the Way.

Also worth considering is the notion that the person who is too stubborn, who leads with his or her authority and has a rigid mind, is likely to fail. Why is that? It is because this person is already old and does not have the leisure to accept other things. The path to success, in contrast, is to be flexible, existing always with possibilities, accepting other possibilities and renewing one's life. Black-and-white logic without flexibility brings about violence and creates a society that does not communicate. But the logic of the gentle middle way that penetrates all things is with us in all things and constantly does its best, creating a society that exists in harmony.

Truth Is like Firing a Bow

The principle of the truth
Is like pulling back a bowstring:
One presses down on the high parts
And lifts the low.
When there is slack, one releases.
Where there is inadequacy, one supplements.

The principle of the truth
Lies in reducing excess
And filling out dearth.

Yet the actions of people are not this way;
They reduce dearth
And devote things where there is excess.

Who might ably contribute excess
To the lacking things in this world?
Only the person who has practiced the truth.
And so
The sage does without boasting,
Achieves without lingering in that place
And does not wish to seem wise.

The Way that is the agent driving the universe is empty, yet it possesses a sense of balance. It raises up that which is too low. It ensures that things that are very deeply hidden see the light of day. Conversely, it makes those who are too active become tired and rest. When we rest for too long, it makes us get up and engage in action. If we look back at history, we see that new, peaceful times have always emerged during times of extreme turbulence, and that when things are well governed, turbulence inevitably comes as a result of one factor or another. All of this could be called the principle of opposites in the truth, its sense of balance. Here, Laozi explains this equitable principle by likening it to the heaven.

Humans seek to give more to the person who is losing his or her sense of balance and to take more from the person who has nothing. This behavior through action is sure to be governed by the truth's law of nonaction.

Instead of letting ourselves be bound by immediate benefit and harm, losses and gains, I think that we should have the eye of truth and an understanding of history, instilling in ourselves the truth's sense of balance as a standard for our own behavior.

When we practice the sort of actions that are the gestures of the truth, by caring for those who lack and sharing strength with those who are struggling, this is the behavior of the sage, and I feel it also helps create the pioneers who will lead the way in building a society of welfare.

Lecture 78

The Great Leaders
of the World

There is nothing in this world that is softer than water,
Nor weaker.
Yet there is nothing that can rival water
In attacking and vanquishing the rigid and strong,
Nor is there anything in the world like water
That can defeat the strong with ease.

So it is
The weak vanquishes the strong,
The soft vanquishes the rigid.

Perhaps there is no one in this world
who does not know,
Yet none who puts it into practice.

The sages have said
The one who accepts the dirt of the country
Is the master of the state.

The one who knows to accept inauspiciousness in a country
Is said to be a great leader of the world.
Such right words
Seem to run counter in this world.

To the person nurturing the virtue of the leader, there may be no better teacher than water. This is why Laozi describes water as being close to the truth. Water is weak and gentle. The leaders of today try to become strong in terms of power, but without substance. When leaders face their various challenges with softness, with the utmost vulnerability, this will build up in them, we are told, and a path will open up for them to overcome powerful challengers.

Water always prepares to land downhill. The most important virtue of a leader is humility and the willingness to lift up others, to learn from them and serve them. A poor leader always tries to stand up before others, to act in a lofty way. In the principles of change in all things, we see that the person who is high and seeks to lead will always be dragged and pulled down. Such a person will face unnecessary challenges, and his or her position will become impossible to sustain. When we volunteer reluctantly and behave humbly, our defending walls will thicken, and we can fend off attacks with ease.

Water accepts the impure and washes all things clean. What a leader needs most urgently is a spirit of service and of generosity. It is predestined by the truth that the leader who sacrifices him- or herself with a mind free of interests, handling the things that others cannot take on, and who leads the way in ushering in a grand design for the next myriad years of his or her country will inevitably be tasked bringing about with great things for that country.

Great Grievances Remain Even after Reconciliation

With great grievances, there remains perforce resentment.

Even after reconciliation,

How can one be said to have done well?

The sage, though he or she may have books of bonds,

Does not hound the indebted.

The person with virtue follows the contract;

The person without virtue collects harshly.

The truth considers no one dearer

Yet exists always with kind people.

Humans do not live alone. They form relationships with many other people. Ordinary people cause more harm to others; the people we describe as "conscientious" share benefits and good things. Sages regard bringing benefits to others as their standard in life.

There is a principle such that while it may be a loss right now to do good things for others, it will come back to us over time. This is the principle of returning, where all things return once they have gone as far as they will. By that principle, what we give will come back to us again. Conversely, the harm we do to others will come back before we know it, harming us equally in turn. Sages are well aware of the principle by which things return. This is what enables them to transcend immediate losses. Of course, the sage is not doing so in a calculated way. The sage gives grace with the state of mind that is no-mind. He or she merely gives grace because of the state of mind of loving-kindness, which regards all living creatures as if they were his or her children.

The truth cannot take anyone's side. Why? Because its functions are always operating from a position of fairness. For that reason, it can never side with anyone. It does, however, grant the laurel wreath of victory to kind people, to people who have accumulated many acts of kindness. This is why this section seems to be saying that the Way exists together with good people.

The Ideal Country Is the Small Country

With small countries and small publics,

Govern with sincerity.

Do not use weapons of war.

Regard the lives of the people as precious

And let them live long in a single place.

Though boats and palanquins may exist, ride them not.

Though there be armor and warriors, do not make camp.

Return to custom bound by twine.

Let them eat sweetly;

Let them dress cleanly;

Let them live in comfort
And enjoy folkways.
Though you may have a border with another country
And you hear the cries of chickens and dogs,
Let there not be coming and going
Until the people age and die.

The country that Laozi regarded as ideal was a somewhat small and trivial one. Here, we should not overlook the fact that these are words from long ago.

A small country, he is saying, is one in which the state can effectively edify the public and train all people in morals, where everyone can live a simple, sincere life and enjoy pleasures together.

A big country suffers from many problems in educating the public; when various social problems arise, they cannot be controlled. To effectively manage and control the problems of today—be they problems with young people, problems with senior citizens, problems with the environment, problems with gender discrimination, or problems with conflict between classes—one's country must be small enough to be managed frugally rather than on a larger scale. Only in a country that small, he tells us, can happiness be brought to far more citizens. A large country might engage in barbaric behavior such as using its abundant power to invade the countries of others. Regarding this, there appear to be many implications when we consider the behavior of the major powers in the world today. Strong countries must in some sense be subdivided more, I feel, and the UN should have an even greater role in establishing order in the world.

If we look at the political and social systems in the small country of Singapore, for example, we can find many more positive aspects, although this is not true for every aspect of the country.

Trustworthy Words Bear
Little Embellishment

Trustworthy words bear little embellishment.

Where there is much embellishment, words cannot be trusted.

The truthful person makes no justifications.

The person who offers excuses

Is lacking truthfulness.

The person who truly knows is not verbose.

The person who is verbose

Cannot be said to know the truth well.

Sages do not accumulate.

The person who serves others
Actually benefits.
The person who gives to others
Is actually enriched.
The path of the truth
Is benefiting all things without doing harm.
The path of the sage
Is offering merits for the world,
Doing without discord.

Words are character.

Words are what communicate a person's thoughts and provide information. Yet when those words bear too much chattiness and rhetoric, they are like a tree that merely has lush leaves and cannot bear fruit. Certain words, we are told here, should have a firm sense, and accurate information should be that of the truth, with no need for embellishment.

Among people who treat words lightly in sensory terms, few of them think deeply, and few of them speak without contradicting themselves. The words of the person who does not think deeply and who contradicts him- or herself from one situation to the next will inevitably hold forth in complicated prose.

Sages value meaning; they do not value expression. They focus more on practice in order to test meaning within reality, and so their expression may appear less than their content.

Ordinary people live through the desire to possess, and so they seek to accumulate objects and to turn those with whom they have affinities into their "own" people. When they cannot have more, they feel anxious and suffer. Sages make embodying the Way the top priority in their lives, and they are so fully absorbed in giving this that they have no time to amass things of their own. Yet no things have a fixed owner. There is a principle by which objects cycle from one moment to the next. Consider the place where you live. The ownership has likely changed hands frequently. The items we possess went from a factory to a wholesaler and on to a retailer before reaching us as consumers, and will be passed on again from us to someone else. Even when we possess something now, it will fall into disrepair and change locations over time.

We must bear in mind the principle of retribution and response of cause and effect: the person who fixates solely on trying to possess will have his or her things taken away, while the person who only gives will only receive from others.

Credits

Author   Prime Dharma Master Kyongsan
Translator   Colin A. Mouat

Publisher   Kim Hyunggeun
Editor   Kim Heesun
Copy editor   Jaime Stief
Proofreader   Anna Bloom
Designer   Kim Jihye